WHAT LEADERS ARE SAYING

about

WALKING WITH LIONS

What if there was more to church life than superficial, see-you-next-Sunday relationships? What if the greatest part of being on a church staff wasn't the important work you got to do, but the radical life-change you experienced as you did it? There is more, and we know it. Yet it often seems elusive, doesn't it? In *Walking With Lions,* Jonathan Wiggins lays out a simple, powerful pathway to richer relationships that I believe will equip you to experience the "more" you're yearning for.

PAUL ANDREW

Lead Pastor of Liberty Church
New York City, New York

For decades, people have heard me say, "Find a need and fill it; find a hurt and heal it." That's our calling in our relationship with unbelievers when we tell them the Good News about Jesus, it's our calling when we serve the poor, and it's our calling in our relationships with one another. In many ways, I think we do better with unbelievers and the poor than we do with those we call brothers and sisters! In *Walking with Lions*, Jonathan Wiggins gives us powerful principles and clear applications so we can genuinely love one another, forgive one another, and accept one another. We'd better not miss this calling! It's a wonderful way to fill needs and heal hurts.

TOMMY BARNETT
Global Pastor of Dream City Church and author of *What If?*
Phoenix, Arizona

Few things in life can have the kind of impact that friendships do. In his book, *Walking with Lions*, my friend Jonathan provides a proven strategy to build a team that you'll not only want around you, but will stick around you.

JOHN BEVERE
Co-founder of Messenger International and Best-Selling Author and Minister
Colorado Springs, Colorado

Many churches do a good job communicating the Word of God but lose sight of the importance of creating healthy and authentic relationships with the family of God. Our spiritual, emotional, and physical well-being depends on our relational health. Jonathan Wiggins has shown us how to deepen and strengthen our "iron sharpening iron" connections with people on our teams and in groups. This is a book worth reading, but even more, it's a book that needs to be the practical guidebook for our most important relationships.

HERBERT COOPER
Senior Pastor of People's Church and author of *But God Changes Everything*
Oklahoma City, Oklahoma

In a day and age where followers are more coveted than friends, Jonathan challenges us to fight for covenantal relationships which were always intended to be a hallmark of the Christian faith. In this book, there is a sense of authenticity and experience because Jonathan actually lives out these principles among his staff and community. This is the type of friend he is to me and so many others. The reward of committing to walk with lions is well worth the risk!

BRANDON CORMIER
Lead Pastor of Zeal Church
Colorado Springs, Colorado

In a society that desperately struggles with how to connect in a healthy and meaningful way, Jonathan Wiggins' new book, *Walking With Lions* is the roadmap to bring life and balance into your relationships. Jonathan is one of the most authentic and generous leaders on the planet. His love and passion for all people is the model that every leader should look to attain. I encourage every pastor and leader to digest this book and apply it to your life.

LEE DOMINGUE
Legacy Pastor at Church of the Highlands, founder of Kingdom Builders USA and author of *Pearls of the King* and *Family Meeting Guide*
Birmingham, Alabama

Jonathan's book is a game changer. Just like the author, it's filled with authentic passion, incredible power and a deep sense of purpose. He masterfully explains the genuine importance of creating and sustaining life-giving relationships in life and leadership. He uncovers the reality of the human condition and its deep need for connection in authentic relationships. I'm better because of this book, and I believe you will be too.

JEREMY FOSTER
Pastor of Hope City Church
Houston, Texas

In *Walking with Lions*, Jonathan elevates an accessible theology of friendship that is both practical and primal, which is so useful as we navigate a culture that has domesticated real relationships. We now settle for relationships that are evident only in the likes and follows we acquire on social media. What we often don't know is that we find the most meaning through those closely assembled around us who are on the same spiritual trajectory—people that are near us and really know us. This book is a recipe for how to create meaningful relationships, and by the time you complete it, you'll have a culture of friendship baked in your DNA.

WAYNE FRANCIS
Lead Pastor of The Life Church
White Plains, New York

Some of life's most difficult challenges can be navigating relationships with other people. In *Walking with Lions*, Jonathan serves as a guide to help you achieve deeper and more meaningful relationships through vulnerability and genuine openness. As you read it, you will find that not only are you inspired personally to carry out the kinds of relationships he describes, but it will overflow to the people you lead. If you care about the kinds of relationships you and those you lead are fostering, you'll grab a copy of this book and read it together.

ROBBY GALLATY
Pastor of Long Hollow Baptist Church
Author of *Growing Up* and *Replicate*
Hendersonville, Tennessee

Jonathan is a one-of-a-kind overcomer who's figured out an ingenious way to choose health while walking through the minefield of Christian leadership. Sadly, many of us don't experience the grace and truth of genuine "one another" relationships. Quite simply, there are a thousand books on WHY we should live authentically, but rare is the book that explains HOW, with profound research and tear-jerking story-telling. It's one of the few books I want my entire leadership team to read. Well done, Jonathan Wiggins!

PETER HAAS
Lead Pastor of SubstanceChurch.com
DJ & Music Producer for SubstanceVariant.com
Minneapolis, Minnesota

In *Walking with Lions*, Jonathan Wiggins blazes a trail for anyone who longs for deeper connections with others while bearing the pain of past disappointments. Grounded by grace and illuminated by God's Word, this book encourages your heart and nourishes your soul like sitting around a campfire with an old friend. You will return to its wisdom again and again.

CHRIS HODGES
Senior Pastor of Church of the Highlands
Author of *The Daniel Dilemma* and *Out of the Cave*
Birmingham, Alabama

I am so grateful that Jonathan Wiggins has shared his pursuit of building stronger relational bonds. There is nothing more important than relationships. Jonathan lovingly provides both principles and practical applications based on his experience and his commitment to live out relationships with his team and others.

PHIL KLEIN
Founder of Focus412
Birmingham, Alabama

Jonathan Wiggins has written one of the most insightful and compelling leadership books of the decade. *Walking with Lions* shows us how we can find courage and strength through relationships. In this book, Jonathan shows us step by step how to delve deeper and foster genuine and enduring relationships with other leaders, propelling us and our leadership teams to higher levels. If you are intentional about becoming the leader God created you to be, then you need this book!

DR. DAVE MARTIN
Success Coach and Pastor
Author of *12 Traits of the Greats*
Detroit, Michigan

As the years go by, each of us realizes how rare and valuable true friendships are, especially true friendships that span the distance of say, 6,838 miles, roughly the distance between Loveland, Colorado and Jerusalem, Israel. Regardless of the physical distance between the worlds of Jonathan Wiggins and myself, I am honored to call him a true friend. The only way this could be possible is by Jonathan "practicing what he preaches" by implementing the principles in this book, among others: transparency, honesty and connectivity. Thank you, Jonathan for continually proving to me, and to many others, that leadership doesn't have to be lonely.

CALEV MYERS
Founder and Chairman of ARISE
Jerusalem

In *Walking With Lions*, Jonathan has given us the necessary tools and equipment to build healthy God honoring relationships. This is not just a book based upon knowledge gleaned from books and research; He has written a book from the place of a true practitioner of healthy relationships.

JASON PARRISH
Lead Pastor of The Well Church
Salt Lake City, Utah

In our world of incredible speed and busyness, it's easy to get caught in the whirlwind of doing and miss out on loving. In his book, Jonathan Wiggins shares how God has led him, his team, and his church to reevaluate how they relate to each other and make the necessary adjustments. In case anyone thinks the kind of powerful, rich relationships he outlines are, well, unnecessary, they need to read the New Testament more carefully. *Walking with Lions* is a template for us to trust God to create life-changing, God-honoring, community-surprising love for each other. To make that happen, we'll need to do some soul-searching, and we'll need to make some adjustments in our priorities. But this, I'm certain, is exactly what God wants us to do.

WENDY PEREZ
Co-Lead Pastor of ChurchLV
Las Vegas, Nevada

All of us have taught and preached about the importance of relationships, and in *Walking with Lions*, Jonathan Wiggins has cracked the code. With the humility born from painful personal experiences and insights gained from years of God's healing touch, he offers hope that church leaders can nurture environments where people connect on a life-changing level. Use this book with your spouse, your best friends, your staff team, and groups in your church . . . and watch God do amazing things!

DINO RIZZO
Executive Director of ARC
Associate Pastor at Church of the Highlands
Author of *Servolution* and *Serve Your City*
Birmingham, Alabama

Everywhere we look, we're surrounded by books offering advice, processes, and plans that promise growth and results. But Pastor Jonathan Wiggins has done something that few do in this day and age of church planting and ministry: he has written a book with a message that stands out among the crowd. *Walking With Lions* takes an important look at leadership and team building from a perspective that is often overlooked—the power of honesty and vulnerability. The truths Jonathan shares have the potential to bring healthy, significant change from the inside out—for you and for those you lead. Furthermore, I believe it can create a ripple effect that can position your team and church for the same authentic connections we in the early church in Acts. When it's present in our teams and churches, we'll see the impact of our churches rise to an even greater level in our communities and beyond.

JOHN SIEBELING

Pastor, The Life Church

Memphis, Tennessee

From the first time I met Jonathan Wiggins a few years back, I have been so impressed with his burning heart for biblical revelation and his service to the body of Christ. I found, not only through our conversations, but also by observing Rez.Church, that Jonathan has divine grace and practical wisdom to deal with leadership issues. This led me to invite him to minister at events aimed towards leaders in Brazil. During the whole time he was with us, we were very enriched. I respect him deeply. I am sure that the divine deposit in his life will overflow through this book and bless your life.

LUCIANO SUBIRA

Founder of Comunidade Alcance

Author of *When Nothing Else Matters* and *The Impact of Holiness*

Curitiba, Brazil

I've watched Jonathan Wiggins walk out the principles from this book. I've seen his own life transformed and witnessed the same in those he has shared them with. I can't wait until a new generation of leaders gets access to the life-giving content that he unfolds. Do yourself a favor and dig in. Your relationships will never be the same.

GREG SURRATT
Founding Pastor of Seacoast Church
President of the Association of Related Churches (ARC) and Author of *Re-Visioning*
Mount Pleasant, South Carolina

We were created to be relational beings, and yet so many of us live isolated lives. We crave genuine relationships and yet often don't know how to really build them. In his book, *Walking With Lions*, Jonathan Wiggins gives us some practical, challenging, real and very helpful steps toward building relationships that have the potential to not only make our lives better, but also make the world a better place.

HOLLY WAGNER
Co-founding Pastor of Oasis Church and Founder of She Rises
Author of *Find Your Brave*
Los Angeles, California

I have had the immense honor of partnering with Jonathan Wiggins in various capacities over the last ten years. He and his wife Amy are incredible people who lead with humility and an eagerness to grow. In his book, *Walking with Lions*, Jonathan gives us tools and a roadmap to walk in greater connection with God and each other. His concepts aren't just theory—he has walked this out with those he leads. I highly recommend this book!

KIM WALKER-SMITH
Singer, Songwriter for the label, Jesus Culture
Sacramento, California

WALKING
WITH LIONS

HOW TO FIND
TRUE COURAGE & ENDURING STRENGTH
THROUGH
GOD-HONORING RELATIONSHIPS

JONATHAN WIGGINS
FOREWORD BY JOHN C. MAXWELL

MY BROTHER RANDALL, ME,
AND OUR COUSIN BRIAN

JULY 1986

NOTHING WITHOUT GOD CELEBRATION → FUNDING CHURCH PLANTERS IN COLORADO
JOSHUA ANDERSON + TONY DOLAND + DRAKE ELKINS + JOSH McGINLEY +
JON BRANNBERG + BRANDON CORMIER + BRADY WRIGHT

MISS MOLLY
& MYSELF

NOVEMBER
1996

(ALTHOUGH SHE LOST
HER VISION AT 21, MISS
MOLLY WAS THE MOST
PERCEPTIVE PERSON
I'VE EVER KNOWN.)

DEDICATION

THIS BOOK IS DEDICATED
TO THE MEMORY OF
Molly Clark Hartrick.

"MISS MOLLY" WAS A FAMILY THERAPIST
WHO WAS INSTRUMENTAL IN HELPING ME
HEAL FROM PAST HURTS.
USING MANY OF THE PRINCIPLES NOW
ARTICULATED IN THIS BOOK.

HER LEGACY OF
**LIGHT + HOPE +
RESTORATION & HEALING**
ENDURES IN MY LIFE AND COUNTLESS OTHERS.

thank you Miss Molly

Unless otherwise noted the version of the Bible used in this book is the NIV.
THE HOLY BIBLE, NEW INTERNATIONAL VERSION®, NIV® Copyright © 1973, 1978, 1984, 2011 by Biblica, Inc.® Used by permission. All rights reserved worldwide.

Scripture marked NCV is taken from the New Century Version®. Copyright © 2005 by Thomas Nelson. Used by permission. All rights reserved.

Scripture marked NLT is taken from the Holy Bible, New Living Translation, copyright © 1996, 2004, 2015 by Tyndale House Foundation. Used by permission of Tyndale House Publishers, Inc., Carol Stream, Illinois 60188. All rights reserved.

Scripture marked NASB is taken from the NEW AMERICAN STANDARD BIBLE®, Copyright © 1960, 1962, 1963, 1968, 1971, 1972, 1973, 1975, 1977, 1995 by The Lockman Foundation. Used by permission.

Scripture marked NKJV is taken from the New King James Version, Copyright © 1982 by Thomas Nelson. Used by permission. All rights reserved.

Scripture marked KJV is from the King James Version, which is in the public domain.

Cover and interior design by Gabi Ferrara at gmadethis.com

ISBN: 978-1-64296-023-5
Published by ARC, The Association of Related Churches
Second printing
Printed in the United States

A PORTION OF THE PROFITS FROM THIS BOOK GO TOWARD PLANTING CHURCHES THROUGH THE ASSOCIATION OF RELATED CHURCHES.

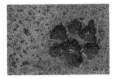
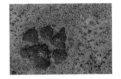
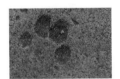

TABLE
of
CONTENTS

FOREWORD

In the two years I've known Jonathan, we've shared hunting trips, many meals, and meaningful conversations. Nothing has been off limits. We've shared our stories, our dreams, and our plans for the future. Early in our relationship, the concepts he shares in this book were forming in his mind, but I could tell he has a God-given gift to distill complex thoughts into principles everyone can grasp and apply. That's what I've been trying to do in my writing for decades, and I appreciate it when I see it in others.

Leadership isn't about positions, and it's not about power; it's about people. We can't lead others without building a relationship with them—a bond based on trust and respect. Without it, nothing is possible . . . with it, all things are possible. All of us want to be effective, but success isn't primarily about sales and market share in business or the number of people in worship on Sundays. The very best leaders understand that the true measure of success is helping other leaders grow, develop, and have a greater impact. And they model the powerful blend of kindness and a bold vision for progress.

I've seen Jonathan's commitment to genuine connections in his relationships with people inside and outside the church. He has waded into conversations with people who were, at first, antagonistic to believers. Too many pastors and other Christians see those outside the body as enemies, or at least nuisances. Jonathan sees them as real people with real hopes and dreams. For him, love knows no bounds.

In *Walking with Lions*, Jonathan explains that people from every background bring something valuable to relationships. Those who have experienced a lifetime of love and encouragement bring security and joy, and those who have suffered heartaches and loss bring the healing they've experienced so that others will be comforted and inspired. Jonathan is in the second group, and I have the greatest admiration for him and people like him.

The process outlined in this book will challenge you to be more honest—first with yourself and God, and then with a few trustworthy people. Following this process produces "an innovative disruption." It changes the nature of relationships by stripping away the facades so that we genuinely know, love, and trust each other more than ever. For those who want richer, stronger, life-affirming yet life-changing relationships, this book is a game-changer. This, I'm convinced, is the way to become a better leader (and spouse and parent and friend).

Jonathan, his wife Amy, and the Rez.Church family are God-given gifts to me. They have partnered with our nonprofit, Equip, which has trained six million leaders around the world, and they're valued partners in our new venture, Transformation, which is designed to have an impact on the leaders in business, government, education, the arts, and medicine in these countries. I'm honored to recommend his book to you. I can't wait to see how God uses Jonathan's message to transform individuals in the church, in families, and even in the business community. God has made us for relationships . . . this book is a gateway to the kind of connections God wants for all of us. Don't miss it!

JOHN C. MAXWELL

Bestselling Author

REZ.CHURCH
10 Year Anniversary Party

CHURCH LEADERSHIP,
FRIENDS & FAMILY

JUNE 19, 2020

INTRODUCTION

Is this possible?
Do the people on our team even want this?
Do I really want this?

These are the questions I asked myself when I came back from a retreat with other pastors and church leaders. On the first day of the four-day event in Montana, I didn't know anyone, but by the end, we'd formed genuine and enduring friendships. I wondered if the process I had just experienced was at all repeatable and transferable. I hoped it was, but I wasn't sure.

Our team was performing and producing at a high level. We had implemented world-class processes, followed the proven models of successful leaders, created engaging worship experiences and used creative strategies to reach our community. We were running on all cylinders as a staff team... still, something seemed to be hollow, missing.

The New Testament paints a multifaceted picture of spiritual growth, including the truth of the Word of God, the power of the Spirit of God, and the encouragement of the people of God. There are, by one scholar's count, fifty-nine "one another" passages. I wondered, *What if we actually lived out those passages on our team? What difference would it make?* That's what I'd experienced at the retreat, and I really wanted our team to have access to the kind of intentionality in building relationships I'd experienced there.

When I first talked to a few key leaders on our team about it, they were, shall we say, less than enthusiastic. I'm sure I didn't explain it completely, so they initially assumed I was asking them to join in something like an emotionally exposing "confession-fest." A couple of them had the guts to express themselves honestly. One told me, "Pastor Jonathan, I don't know if I want to risk being transparent with you on a personal level . . . After all, you're the guy who has the power to fire me." Another asked, "Do you really think we'll be completely honest about the junk in our lives when the people listening are in the offices down the hall—and we see them every day?" To me, these seemed like legitimate comments that deserved good responses.

Consequently, I developed a very clear plan and process that would empower my team at Rez to pursue this process on their terms and at their pace. I sent each one an invitation to engage with me in what became a five-step process:

✸ RELATE + TRUST + DISCLOSE + PROCESS + INTEGRATE ✸

One by one, each person on the team accepted the invitation and engaged in the steps I had laid out for us. Later, a couple of them told me they'd had very limited expectations. They thought the process might lead to a stimulating conversation or two, some helpful leadership advice, or an encouraging pep talk that would energize them to perform better. But the results, we all discovered, were infinitely more valuable.

Over time something really powerful began to happen: we had conversations we'd never imagined before. Nothing was forced and no one was "guilted" to say more than they wanted to, but as trust was built, each of us peeled off layers of self-protection that had kept others from really knowing us. We began to disclose areas of our lives that few people, if any, knew about us—our struggles, failures, doubts, questions, shame, and the inner-life that we had worked so hard to conceal, outperform, and will our way out of. We had all experienced "church accountability" before, but this was different. This wasn't just a session of gut-wrenching confession to get something off of our chest and then a quick prayer. This was a gradual process of choosing to live in the light of genuine community and the power of the Spirit. We were experiencing the grace of the "one another" life so often encouraged in the Scriptures.

We spent many hours engaging in this process. It was challenging, rewarding, humbling, stimulating, disarming, and empowering. The walls of compartmentalization that we had carefully constructed over decades began to feel unnecessary and unhelpful. As those walls came down, we were enabled to live the kind of integrated life that God wants for us... catalyzing growth like we'd never known.

WE WERE EXPERIENCING THE GRACE OF THE "ONE ANOTHER" LIFE SO OFTEN ENCOURAGED IN THE SCRIPTURES.

The ripple effect has been amazing. People on the team have repeatedly told me that their honesty and security has had an impact on their marriages, their relationships with their children, their leadership of their ministry teams, and their friendships inside and outside the church. The people who office next to us are no longer just coworkers. They're brothers in arms who truly know us, fight for us, protect us, challenge us, and above all, love us. Isolation began to disappear. The individual departments were no longer islands. Our production as a team increased beyond what great leadership methodology alone could produce. We were united not only in mission, but in heart.

My wife Amy led our female team leaders through the same process with great success. The process outlined in this book has become a very effective empowerment mechanism for the women on our team.

Eventually, my team of guys carved out times to go to the mountains together for our own version of the Montana retreat. During one of our trips, a leader who facilitated team building for our group compared the healthy and powerful alliances we were forming to a pride of lions. "Lions run with lions" was a phrase that resonated with us, and we began to call ourselves "the lions." After the trip, one of the men from our team gave each of us a wood carving that reads, **"All of my friends are lions."**

I thought of nature programs that show how lions work together to capture their prey. There are risks for a lion living in a group and hunting together with other powerful creatures, but lone lions don't make it very long. Neither do lone leaders. It takes courage to be a lion in a group. That's our team's commitment, and because of it we are all better, stronger, and healthier.

Let this book serve as a roadmap, an inspiration, and an invitation for you to walk with lions.

THE GREATEST FEAR IN THE WORLD IS

THE OPINION OF OTHERS.

AND THE MOMENT YOU ARE

UNAFRAID OF THE CROWD

YOU ARE NO LONGER A SHEEP.

YOU BECOME A LION.

✹

A GREAT ROAR

ARISES IN YOUR HEART.

THE ROAR OF FREEDOM.

LIONS
RUN
with
LIONS.

— BRIAN CARPENTER —

THE REFUGE
Fort Scott, Kansas

JOSHUA BOYETT
ZACH SANCHEZ
LANDON HAIRGROVE

MAY 2020

2016

FAMILY VACATION TO DISNEY WORLD
WITH AMY + MADELYN + SARAH + SAMUEL

CHAPTER ONE

CREATED TO CONNECT

Years ago, my wife Amy and I decided to blow our entire IRS refund on our first trip to Disney World for us and our kids. We had a blast! We rode every ride and ate at every shop—at least, that's the way it seemed—and we had our pictures taken with all the characters. I rode the Tower of Terror with the kids. (Amy opted out of that one.) We screamed at the drops and held our breath with wide-eyed anticipation on the lifts. We even enjoyed waiting in the long lines because we talked incessantly about what was coming next. Nothing could stop us from having the time of our lives. Disney instantly became an integral element in our family's DNA.

A few years later, Amy said, "I'd like to go to Disneyland, but just with you this time."

I responded, "Awesome! Let's do it."

Again, I wanted to ride the Tower of Terror (renamed Guardians of the Galaxy — Mission: Breakout!), and again, Amy said she had better things to do than self-imposed torture. She doesn't even like elevators, and this ride... well, it's a little more intense than standing in an elevator. She found something else to do as I got in line, but this time, there was no one to talk to, no one to laugh with, and no one to share the anticipation of the thrill of the ride. I was bored and I felt alone in a crowd of people at "the happiest place on earth." In my self-imposed silence, I overheard the conversation of some college-age kids in front of me. In fact, they were about the age of my oldest son, Nathan. Something in my brain must have unconsciously shifted because I gradually identified something about them with my children. One of the girls made a joke, and we all laughed. That's the point: we . . . *all* . . . laughed. She turned and glared at me with a stink-eye as if to say, "You are such a creep!" I turned away and tried to act like not-a-creep! (That's harder to do than you might imagine.) Thankfully, they ignored me the rest of the weeks we were in line together. (Okay, it was only about fifteen more minutes, but it seemed like weeks.) I wanted to disintegrate or evaporate because being near those kids felt so incredibly awkward.

And I didn't enjoy the ride, either. The whole experience fell flat because there was no one to share it with me.

KNOWN AND LOVED — THE HOPE AND THE RISK

God has made us relational creatures. We like to put people into two categories: extroverts and introverts, but I'm afraid many people misunderstand these concepts. When psychiatrist Carl Jung originally coined the terms, he put them as ends of a long continuum, and he insisted that no one is on the extremes. In other words, all of us have some characteristics of both. Still, it's helpful to understand the difference between the two sides of the spectrum. It's not that extroverts enjoy people and introverts prefer to be alone. That's the common misunderstanding. Instead, think of it as answering the question: How are people charged and recharged? People who lean toward the extrovert side get energy from being with people, and their energy fades when they spend too much time alone. Conversely, those who lean toward the introvert side enjoy being with people, but not too many, too long, or too often. Their levels of creativity and energy rise when they're alone (or perhaps with only one or two people) long enough to think, read, plan, and pray. Extroverts and introverts are electric cords looking for a socket, but they're looking for different sockets.

My point is that people at both extremes have an innate desire, a need, and maybe even a compulsion to be thoroughly known and deeply loved—both, not one or the other. They may express and receive love in different ways, but the need is powerful and immediate in both of them. Author and pastor Tim Keller observes, "To be loved but not known is comforting but superficial. To be known and not loved is our greatest fear. But to be fully known and truly loved is, well, a lot like being loved by God. It is what we need more than anything. It liberates us from pretense, humbles us out of our self-righteousness, and fortifies us for any difficulty life can throw at us." [1]

> ## DEEP IN ALL OUR HEARTS LURKS THE FEAR OF BEING ALONE. TO FEEL ALIENATED AND ISOLATED IS TORTURE.

Deep in all our hearts lurks the fear of being alone. To feel alienated and isolated is torture. Even the most hardened criminals are afraid of solitary confinement, and those who suffer this kind of punishment are often affected long after they reenter the prison population. A report by the American Psychological Association concludes that the nation's 80,000 prisoners in solitary confinement "are at grave risk of psychological harm." A man who spent eighteen years in prison, including ten in solitary, for a murder he didn't commit, explains, "I would watch guys come to prison totally sane, and in three years they don't live in the real world anymore." Doctor and professor Craig Haney concludes, "One of the very serious psychological consequences of solitary confinement is that it renders many people incapable of living anywhere else. They actually get to the point where they become frightened of other human beings." When they are released, either back into the prison population or out of prison, they may have difficulty functioning because they're overwhelmed with anxiety caused by prolonged relational disconnection.[2]

Some people have told me they're "not wired" the way other people are, so they don't need relationships. For them and many others, there's a corollary fear: the fear of being exposed. They're convinced that if other people knew what's really in their hearts, and if they knew what terrible things they'd done, they'd run away as fast as they could!

I understand the terror associated with being known but not loved. People have developed elaborate ways to "pose" and look secure when they're terribly afraid of anyone seeing below the surface. In his classic book, *The Four Loves*, C. S. Lewis warned that the fear of exposure carries its own risks:

> To love at all is to be vulnerable. Love anything and your heart will be wrung and possibly broken. If you want to make sure of keeping it intact you must give it to no one, not even an animal. Wrap it carefully round with hobbies and little luxuries; avoid all entanglements. Lock it up safe in the casket or coffin of your selfishness. But in that casket, safe, dark, motionless, airless, it will change. It will not be broken; it will become unbreakable, impenetrable, irredeemable. To love is to be vulnerable. [3]

And to be loved is liberating. Tommy Walker is a songwriter and performer who was asked by his pastor to write a song to go with a sermon titled, "He

Knows My Name." The text for the message was Jesus' familiar assurance in John 10: "The gatekeeper opens the gate for him, and the sheep listen to his voice. He calls his own sheep by name and leads them out. When he has brought out all his own, he goes on ahead of them, and his sheep follow him because they know his voice" (John 10:3-4). Walker wrote the song, but he didn't like it very much. He called it "my feeble little act of finishing what I started."

Sometime later, Walker flew to the Philippines to serve at an orphanage on a short-term missions trip. There he met a seven-year-old boy named Jerry. Every day, Jerry asked him, "Tommy, what's my name?" And every day, Walker looked him in the eyes, smiled, and said, "Your name is Jerry." In recalling those encounters, he remembers, "I have to say, not many people on this earth knew this abandoned, extremely poor boy's name—but I got to tell him that someone much greater then me did, and I got to sing to him and many of his orphan friends this song."[4] I think all of us are at least a little bit like Jerry. We want someone to know us, remember us, and call us by name.

To a great extent, all of us live in the tension between the fear of not being known and the fear of being exposed. We try to cope with the tension in a myriad of ways, and many of us never find a truly safe person who knows the worst about us and loves us still. We can feel alone and unwanted in any size crowd, from two to two thousand. To be isolated is to try to look powerful and confident, but to feel invisible, to remain unknown, to feel insignificant, to put our passion to make a difference on the shelf . . . but to act like everything is "just fine."

We face real risks when we take a step to be vulnerable. I remember telling my friend (and part of our group of lions) Sethry Connor something about myself that I'd never told anyone else. As soon as I told him, I realized I was more exposed than I'd ever been. I quickly blurted out, "I'm not sure we can be friends after this!" I wondered if he'd shake his head in disgust, laugh, or find the nearest door. Thankfully, he didn't do any of those things. He listened, asked some great questions, listened even more, and encouraged me. And he shared some things with me that he'd never told anyone. I wondered if I'd have a "vulnerability hangover" the next day. Would I feel ashamed and exposed? Had I given Sethry ammunition to shoot me down when I wasn't expecting an attack? Would I suffer from "confessor's remorse"? Would either or both of us avoid eye contact and try to act like we'd never had the conversation? (Do these questions sound like I was paranoid? No, I'm just being honest about what I was afraid might happen.) Again, my fears were relieved. We affirmed each other and consolidated the gains we'd made. Over time, Sethry and I developed a sense of brotherhood and close friendship that has made us both better men, fathers, husbands, leaders, and Christ-followers. Each step has been a risk, and each step has been liberating.

> THERE'S NOTHING TRANSCENDENT ABOUT LONELINESS. THERE'S NO NOBEL PRIZE FOR LIVING BEHIND WALLS TO PROTECT OURSELVES FROM BEING HURT.

But we also take risks when we don't connect with people at a deeper level. We use people instead of loving them. They don't appreciate being pressured so they leave, and we experience a significant churn on our teams. We're poor models of the gospel to the people in our churches, and people outside the church see us as just another organization trying to grow instead of genuinely demonstrating the heart of Jesus. The risk, then, cuts both ways, but on balance, it's wise to side with Jesus and take the risk to know and love people.

There's nothing transcendent about loneliness. There's no Nobel Prize for living behind walls to protect ourselves from being hurt. We make the wrong kind of difference when we intimidate people to have control over them because we're so insecure. We're less than honest when we act like chameleons, changing what we say and do to please the person in front of us at the moment. The hole in our hearts remains a chasm if we achieve great success but we aren't in relationships where we're loved and we love in return.

We're made for relationships.

DOES IT MATTER?

Many studies have been conducted to determine the effects of healthy, affirming relationships, and the results are unambiguous. Two Harvard studies are representative. The first cites a study in Sweden with people over seventy-five which concluded that the risk of dementia is lowest among those who have strong, satisfying relationships with family and friends. The study found that positive social connections give us pleasure, but relationships also have observable long-term health benefits "every bit as powerful as adequate sleep, a good diet, and not smoking. . . . Conversely, a relative lack of social ties is associated with depression and later-life cognitive decline, as well as with increased mortality. One study, which examined data from more than 309,000 people, found that lack of strong relationships increased the risk of premature death from all causes by 50%—an effect on mortality risk roughly comparable to smoking up to 15 cigarettes a day, and greater than obesity and physical inactivity." [5]

A second Harvard report is from a longitudinal study begun during the Great Depression and continuing for eighty years. It looked at contrasting results between men who had been students at Harvard (because there were no women at the school when the study began) and urban men and women. The study found that close, affirming human connections are the most important factor in physical, mental, and psychological health. The report is titled "Good Genes Are Nice, but Joy Is Better," and states, "Close relationships, more than money or fame, are what keep people happy throughout their lives. . . . Those ties protect people from life's discontents, help to delay mental and physical decline, and are better predictors of long and happy lives than social class, IQ, or even genes. That finding proved true across the board among both the Harvard men and the inner-city participants." [6]

So, here's the truth: it doesn't matter if you're rich or poor, fit or unhealthy, native or immigrant, powerful or powerless, young or old—meaningful relationships are the most important thing in life.

FROM THE BEGINNING

We don't have to read very far in the Bible to find the importance of relationships. In the creation account in the first chapter of Genesis, we see the refrain, "And God said . . . And God saw that it was good." The crowning glory of those six days was the creation of a being, Adam, who was unlike anything else that had been made, a man made in the very image of God. And God was in an intimate relationship with him.

Why did God create Adam? Was God lonely? Augustine explained that if God were unipersonal, He would have had to create somebody to give and receive love, but the Trinity shows that the Father, Son, and Holy Spirit were loving each other for all of eternity.[7] God didn't create people because He was lonely; He created us because He wanted to share His love with us.

Yet in the next chapter of Genesis, we find Adam working in the Garden, but this time, God said, "It is not good for the man to be alone. I will make a helper suitable for him" (Genesis 2:18). What in the world was "not good"? Adam lived in a perfect environment, had never sinned, was given a meaningful role, and had close communication with the Creator—but there was still something missing. God had created Adam to thrive only when he experienced both a vertical relationship with Him and horizontal relationships with people, and specifically, Eve. God created her and put her in front of Adam, who exclaimed, "This is now bone of my bones and flesh of my flesh" (Genesis 2:23). Many commentators think this was a song. In other words, the Bible opens with a nude man singing Michael Bublé to a nude woman. My friend, it doesn't get any more vulnerable and wonderful than that!

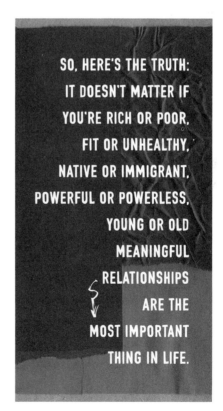

SO, HERE'S THE TRUTH: IT DOESN'T MATTER IF YOU'RE RICH OR POOR, FIT OR UNHEALTHY, NATIVE OR IMMIGRANT, POWERFUL OR POWERLESS, YOUNG OR OLD MEANINGFUL RELATIONSHIPS ARE THE MOST IMPORTANT THING IN LIFE.

We know the story of their catastrophic fall into sin, and immediately, the first couple sewed fig leaves to cover themselves, and "hid from the Lord God

"

BEING ALONE MAY NOT SEEM BAD. BUT IT CERTAINLY ISN'T GOOD.

among the trees of the garden" (Genesis 3:8). People have been ashamed and hiding ever since. When God confronted them, Adam told Him, "I heard you in the garden, and I was afraid because I was naked, so I hid." His nudity hadn't been a problem before. When God asked if he had disobeyed and had eaten from the forbidden tree, Adam performed the fine art of blame-shifting: "The woman you put here with me—she gave me some fruit from the tree, and I ate it" (Genesis 3:10-12). Boom! "It's not my fault! It's Eve's fault . . . and Yours because You gave her to me!" Eve then joined the game by blaming the serpent instead of owning her responsibility (Genesis 3:13).

In this story, we see two kinds of isolation: passive and active. When Adam was working in the Garden before Eve came along, he was doing exactly what he was created to do. He wasn't lonely because he or his environment was somehow defective. Being alone may not seem bad, but it certainly isn't good. He needed human connections. But after the fall, Adam and Eve experienced active isolation. They covered up, hid, and blamed others.

I've noticed both kinds of isolation in my life. I can sometimes be isolated because I'm engrossed in a project, writing a message, or preoccupied with planning. I've learned that it's not good for me to be passively isolated very long. It's far more problematic when I actively isolate: blaming others, minimizing a problem, excusing myself for bad behavior, or denying any problem even exists. When I've hurt someone or I'm upset with somebody, my natural inclination is to avoid them, and my tendency to hide isn't limited to unresolved tension. A few years ago when a high school reunion approached, I thought long and hard (in other words, I was anxious) about how much weight I've gained, and how my appearance and career would compare with the old friends I'd see. I thought about not going, but instead, I crafted a plan to present an attractive image. I was sewing fig leaves. When I experience active isolation in any of its forms, I need someone to do for me what God did for Adam and Eve—call me out so I can begin the process of restoration, healing, and growth.

Before the creation, the Father, Son, and Holy Spirit enjoyed a perfect relationship of love. God's intention for human beings was to replicate and extend that kind of connection between us and Him and among ourselves, but since the Garden, relationships where we feel totally known and deeply loved have proved elusive. In their place, we've pursued "lesser gods" of power, possessions, and prestige, which promise fulfillment but eventually leave us empty and confused.

WORTH IT

From countless conversations about relationships, I've concluded that everyone, introverts and extroverts, are designed for meaningful connections. Most of us want an ironclad guarantee that if we take the risk to be even a little bit vulnerable, the person will affirm us instead of betraying us. But relationships always involve a measure of risk. The questions are: Who is trustworthy? What's the first step? And is it really worth the risk?

We live in a web of human connections: our parents and siblings, people at work, neighbors, people at church, friends, and our own families. We keep many if not most of these people at arm's length, in many cases for very good reasons. But we need at least one person we trust enough to take one step toward vulnerability. We don't need twenty, and we may not find more than one, but one is enough, at least at the beginning. Solomon wrote, "One who has unreliable friends soon comes to ruin, but there is a friend who sticks closer than a brother" (Proverbs 18:24). That's what I've found, and that's my hope for you—that you'll find a true friend, someone who loves without strings attached, is available, and imparts equal measures of grace and truth.

Most of us have built-in resistance to this depth of relationships. We've been deeply hurt before, and we certainly don't want to be hurt again. Some are haunted by secrets we've never told a soul. Some are naïve and trust untrustworthy people, and are disappointed again and again. Some of us are driven and busy, and we don't want any distractions. And some have become numb to our deep longing for a rich, real friendship.

Recognize your hurts and hopes, your longing and your resistance. Acknowledge the passive isolation of busyness and the active isolation which is the product of the fear of exposure. You have to know where you are to have an idea of where you want to go.

In this book, I want to provide clear steps forward. All of them can be summarized like this: Find a trustworthy person, weigh the risks, and take a step away from hiding and toward vulnerability...just one step. The more we're known and loved, the more we can live powerfully, honestly, confidently, and increasingly free from shame, fear, regrets, and self-imposed limitations.

The message of this book is for individuals, small groups, teams, couples, families, mentors, and friends. I'm not asking anyone to take a giant leap from isolation to complete vulnerability. I'm only encouraging each of us to take one step, and when we feel more secure, to take another one. I want the principles in this book to lower the level of risk so we can gradually create the kind of relationships that transform lives.

MY PROMISE

I promise that I'm not going to push you to do anything you don't want to do. Each step is completely up to you. Trust is the currency of relationships, and for many, their trust account is deep in the red. It has been shattered by the trauma of abuse, or it has been gradually eroded by a thousand minimizing, degrading voices. Relationships can only go as deep as trust has been established, and trust must be earned; it can't be demanded. Trust is built or restored slowly as people prove they're worthy of trust.

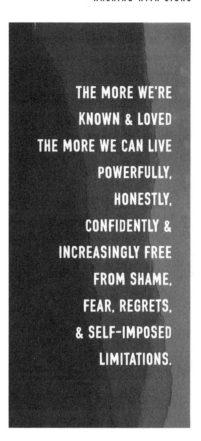

THE MORE WE'RE KNOWN & LOVED THE MORE WE CAN LIVE POWERFULLY, HONESTLY, CONFIDENTLY & INCREASINGLY FREE FROM SHAME, FEAR, REGRETS, & SELF-IMPOSED LIMITATIONS.

In this book, I'll tell my story and share the principles I've learned about creating stronger, deeper, richer relationships on a team and throughout a church, but this isn't the only way to do it. You may find other authors and teachers who have the same goal but a different process. Whether you use my book or theirs, do whatever it takes to create this kind of culture. It matters . . . it matters a lot.

Let me give you a quick overview of where we're going: The first six chapters set the stage. They're an invitation (a long but important one) to evaluate your eagerness or reluctance to trust and consider how trust can be earned. The last six chapters outline practical steps to have richer, stronger relationships.

Isn't that what you want? Isn't that why you're reading this book?

JACKIE AND ERNIE

Let me end the chapter with this story: Jackie and her husband Ernie were an older couple who attended our church. I didn't know them very well, but when I found out he had died, I went to see her. She asked me to speak at his funeral, and I felt honored. Instead of preaching sermons at funerals, I've made it a practice to interview family members and tell their stories about the one they love. When I met with Jackie, she told me a beautiful love story. When Ernie was fifteen, he faked his ID so he could get a pilot's license. He soon learned the skill of crop-dusting. She was fascinated by this daring, handsome young man, and they fell in love. Probably in his very best Humphrey Bogart voice, he told her, "Stick with me, kid. We're going places!" They got married, and a few years later they traveled all over the world as he taught pilots to fly crop dusters.

At one point, they lived in Kenya. They had an agreement that if Ernie saw something interesting on his flight that day—like lions, elephants, herds of wildebeests, or something equally amazing—he'd fly low over their duplex so she'd know to meet him at the airfield. A crop duster has only one seat, so he put a Pepsi crate behind the pilot's seat where she could sit and look out the window. Each time they flew together, the sun was setting, and Ernie showed Jackie amazing sights she would never forget. I can picture the two of them in that tiny cockpit, smiling as they soared over the plains full of exotic animals.

Many years later when they retired, Ernie built their dream home in Florida. As Jackie finished telling me their story, she sat back and smiled. She reminisced, "Ernie made so many of my dreams come true."

At that moment, I realized I didn't even know what Amy's dreams were, or my kids' dreams, or my best friends' dreams, because I'd never asked.

I went home that night and began conversations with Amy and the children about their highest hopes and biggest dreams. We did some pretty crazy things to fulfill them, including buying an RV and putting 25,000 miles on it in the first year. We went places we'd always wanted to go but had seldom if ever told each other about.

I could have gone through the motions to do Ernie's funeral, but asking Jackie to tell me their love story impacted my life, opened my eyes, and showed me the beauty of two people who were far more than roommates. God has created us for connections. You need at least one true friend who always lets you in but never lets you down—or at least, that's the intention. [8]Can you find that person? Will you be that person for someone else? As the friendships on our staff team have developed and deepened, we began to call ourselves "lions" because it implies courage. It takes courage to stop posing and begin living in truth. Maybe you'll find a group of lions to run with. That's my hope for you.

At the end of each chapter, you'll find some questions designed to encourage personal reflection and stimulate discussion. Don't rush through these. Take time to think, pray, talk, and identify your next steps.

THE WIGGINS FAMILY
1985

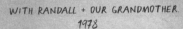

WITH RANDALL + OUR GRANDMOTHER
1978

DISNEYLAND
JANUARY 2020

*reflect on
what
you've
read*

consider THIS

1

Who knows your dreams?

....

....

....

....

....

....

....

....

2

Whose dreams do you know and value? Whose dreams do you need to know better?

....

....

....

....

....

....

....

....

3

Describe the similarities
and differences
between passive and
active isolation.

....

....

....

....

....

....

....

....

....

....

4

What are ways you've
seen people try
to cope with their
sense of isolation?

....

....

....

....

....

....

....

....

....

....

5

Have you experienced
the fear of being known
but not loved, or the
emptiness of being
loved but not known?
Explain your answer.

....
....
....
....
....
....
....
....
....

6

What do you hope to
get out of this book?

....
....
....
....
....
....
....
....
....
....

MY SCHOOL PHOTO —> 1982

THE WICKED FLEE

THOUGH

NO ONE PURSUES,

BUT THE

righteous

ARE AS

BOLD

AS A LION.

— PROVERBS 28:1 —

CHAPTER TWO

WALLS, GATES, AND MACHINE GUNS

It only takes one.

A friend of mine, I'll call him James, was a senior vice president of a tech company. Over the years, the management team grew very close and became best friends. It was, he often told me, a wonderful place to work. At one point, one of the executives retired. My friend was put in charge of the search team, and they hired a company to assist them in finding just the right person for the job. They wanted someone who would fit their team's culture as well as bring expertise to the role. After an extensive search and rounds of interviews, they believed they had the right person. Marsha was hired and welcomed to the team.

The first few months went very smoothly. Marsha enjoyed the camaraderie and banter of the team, and she seemed to appreciate their honesty and vulnerability. James, the president, and the rest of the team didn't realize, however, that Marsha was compiling a catalog of private information she learned as people shared—and they were blindsided when she used it against them. She began with subtle threats in the form of passive-aggressive comments that signaled she might use her confidential knowledge to embarrass other team members. She laughed when she said it, but that's the thing about passive-aggressive behavior—it looks innocent, but it's deadly.

One day the president announced that Marsha was being promoted to be one of the vice presidents in charge of a department. James immediately went to his office and asked for an explanation, but the president would only say, "I had to do it. I'm sorry, but I had to."

Over the next six weeks, several members of the team resigned or were fired, including James. The president developed a heart condition and was sidelined for a month. The person left in charge? Marsha, of course.

How could one person wreck the strong relationships of an entire team? Believe me, it happens in business, the church, families, and among neighbors and friends. When we're young, many of us assume people will be supportive as we enter the work world, like our friends have been. Our sky-high expectations make the crash of reality even more devastating. This chapter is a clear-eyed look at what happens when mistrust and manipulation occur.

Someone who was speaking the truth about this problem was told, "You're so negative!"

He responded, "Well, I'm positive these things are true!"

Indeed, they are. People are very creative in finding ways to cope with the hurt, shame, and disappointment they experience. I know. I've been there.

MISS MOLLY

My father planted a church in a small town in Louisiana. I'm the youngest of three kids. Like the experience of many people, our home could have been labeled "dysfunctional." My dad was prone to outbursts of anger; my mother worked twelve hours a day, and when she was at home, she was exhausted. I felt very insecure. I internalized all of my painful emotions, and my conclusion—my inescapable conclusion—was that I must have been a very bad person. That was the only way to explain my father's anger and my mother's inability to protect me.

I had a tremendous amount of hurt, fear, anger, and shame, but I couldn't admit to any of it. If anyone had asked if I felt anger toward my dad, I would have instantly answered, "No, not at all. I don't know what you're talking about."

When I went to school, my fear and pain drove me to please people, especially my teachers. I lived to win a smile from them. Their approval, their kind words, their pats on the shoulder were what I wanted more than anything in the world. I was a sensitive boy, and I acquired the skill of reading people so I could say just the right words and do just the right thing to please them.

My other defense was isolation. I felt very uncomfortable in groups, so I drifted away and spent a lot of time alone. I saw kids make fun of others, pick on people, and talk behind their backs, and those moments made me feel far too vulnerable. I played baseball and soccer, and I was okay out in the field, but hanging around the other boys in the dugout or the sidelines raised my level of anxiety.

My two childhood coping strategies are obvious now: I pleased people to win their love, and I isolated to feel safe.

When I told someone my story, he asked, "Where was your mother during all this?"

I answered, "She was there but not there. When I was a boy, I didn't understand why she didn't protect me." Before she passed away, I asked her that question, and she told me that my dad was very harsh with her, and she was afraid of his anger, too.

My dad's summer camp was a few miles from our church. He asked an old friend, Molly Hartrick, who was a family therapist who lived nearby, to step in to care for troubled kids who came to the camp. She was blind, but she was incredibly perceptive. By the time I was sixteen, Miss Molly had been a regular at the camp for eight years. That summer, my emotional cauldron finally boiled over, and I couldn't take living at home any longer. I ran away to my best friend's house. When my father found out I was gone, he came after me. I guess I wasn't ready for the CIA because I was at the first place my father looked for me. He insisted I get in the car with him.

As we sped along the highway, my dad was obviously very angry, and I wondered how much worse it would be when we got home. I said, "We need to go see Miss Molly." I was looking for an intervention.

For some reason, Dad agreed. Instead of driving toward our home, he turned to go to Miss Molly's. I'm sure he couldn't imagine that I would actually tell her the truth, so he felt safe enough for us to see her together. In a few minutes, we arrived at her home in Bastrop.

Miss Molly welcomed us and invited us to sit in her home counseling office. Immediately, Dad started talking, but after only a minute or two, she waved to stop him. She turned to me and said, "Jonathan, why don't you tell me what's going on?"

I looked at my father. He was shaking his head with the clear message that if I told her the truth, I'd be in big trouble. I was past that. It was time to be honest with somebody, and I trusted Miss Molly. I took a deep breath and said, "I ran away. I ran because my dad's anger is out of control." Miss Molly was a little lady, barely over five feet tall, but she had a formidable expression, one that communicated both strength and kindness. It's a little odd to say that a blind person had "that look," but she did. I felt safe with her. She asked me a few questions, but she didn't need many specifics.

During this conversation, my dad's expression wilted from fierce intimidation to calm resignation. I'd never seen him that way before. He had always escalated, but now he was deflated. Miss Molly asked me to leave the room. She had a conversation with my dad, but I didn't hear a word. He was exposed . . . and embarrassed. He never severely punished me again.

I left home to live with another family, and Miss Molly gave me a year of free counseling. She was a wonderful listener, and I poured my heart out to her. At one point, I told her, "I don't ever want to be like my father!"

She smiled and said with a voice full of wisdom, "My desire for you, Jonathan—and I wonder if this is your desire, too—is for you to be the person God wants you to be."

"Of course, that's what I want," I told her, "but I don't know how to do that!"

She explained, "It starts with forgiveness."

I knew that forgiving my father would be the most difficult—and the most necessary—thing I would ever do. It didn't seem right to forgive him, but I knew I had to if I would ever be free from the shame and pain.

She explained that forgiveness is part of the healing process. Like a broken bone, when emotional wounds are healed, they become the strongest part of us. She told me, "You can be stronger *because* you were broken." That was a benefit I'd never imagined, and it was very appealing. My deepest hurts could, under the transforming hand of a kind and loving God, become something of a superpower. For the first time, I began to grasp the meaning of Paul's profession: "Therefore I will boast all the more gladly about my weaknesses, so that Christ's power may rest on me. That is why, for Christ's sake, I delight in weaknesses, in insults, in hardships, in persecutions, in difficulties. For when I am weak, then I am strong" (2 Corinthians 12:9-10). But first, I had to do the hard work of forgiving my father for hurting me and my mom for not protecting me.

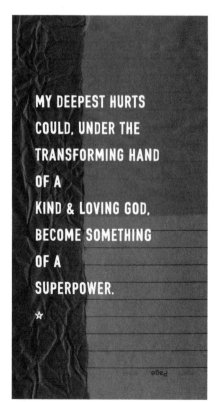

MY DEEPEST HURTS COULD, UNDER THE TRANSFORMING HAND OF A KIND & LOVING GOD, BECOME SOMETHING OF A SUPERPOWER.

Today, with the benefit of decades of hindsight, I understand that my father's upbringing shaped him in ways I couldn't comprehend when I was a boy. His father was verbally abusive, humiliating and berating my dad with cruel, angry words. In addition, the spiritual environment of his family and their church was full of terror and shame, resulting in years of emotional instability. I believe my dad had many good intentions as a father and did many good things for his children, but he was a product of family and religious dysfunction and abuse. He has since expressed profound remorse and sadness for the hurt he caused, and I have forgiven him. Family pain tends to be passed on from generation to generation until there is an intentional course correction. That has been my direction and my goal—to pass love, kindness, affection, and delight to my children.

I'm sure doctors can describe in detail how a broken bone heals, but emotional broken bones heal in fits and starts. It's always a process. God, in His grace, doesn't show us all the pain at once, or we'd be overwhelmed. Over time, He gives us moments, conversations, experiences, and insights that gradually allow us to grieve the losses, forgive the offenders, and heal the deep hurts.

During the process, it was certainly a temptation for me, and I understand it is for most others, to slide into self-pity from time to time. It feels so right! We see ourselves as "the one who was wronged," so we feel completely justified in seeing ourselves as victims and resenting those who hurt us. But it's a self-absorbed quagmire. God brought me some wonderfully loving and blunt friends, like Larry and Ann Brock, to say things like, "Hey Jonathan, is feeling sorry for yourself your thing? Is that working for you? Quit acting like a victim. You won't get anywhere doing that! Respect yourself and follow your calling." And they were right.

Healing and forgiving are choices and processes. Like a person with a broken leg who makes choices to have surgery and go to rehab, we choose to forgive, but forgiveness always involves a measure of grieving what we've lost . . . and that takes time.

When I talk to people about the importance of finding people to trust, and they're resistant, I understand their fears. I understand because I've lived them.

MACHINE GUNS AND TRAMPLED FENCES

The field of counseling has given us many different handles on the ways people respond to stress, abuse, and abandonment. The family systems approach identifies specific roles people play, including hero, clown, rescuer, scapegoat, and switchboard.[9] Cognitive behavioral therapy is based on the premise that psychological, emotional, and relational problems originate in faulty patterns of thinking. Their solution is to identify and reject self-defeating thoughts and replace them with the truth.[10] (Many Christian counselors advocate this model.) The Karpman Drama Triangle identifies three "stances" people take in stress-filled relationships — rescuer, victim, and persecutor — and they switch from one to the other to control other people on the triangle.[11] Similarly, in *The Wounded Heart*, Dan Allender observes three primary ways people, particularly women, cope with sexual abuse: they take on the persona of the Good Girl, the Party Girl, or the Tough Girl.[12]

You may want to shout, "Jonathan, have you lost your mind? Are you saying secular psychology is valuable?" The answer to the first question is that the jury is probably still out, but the answer to the second is, "Yes, with some qualifications." The wide field of psychology often excels at describing the causes and the results of mental health problems. A few

Christian psychologists do a great job with this analysis, but many believers are too simplistic, which can leave them feeling even more discouraged and ashamed when the promises of quick cures don't happen. The secular models are long on identifying the problem, but they're short on the remedy. They have some very helpful principles, but they don't point to the powerful, life-changing experience of rightly applying the *Word of God*, the transforming power of the *Spirit of God*, the nurturing effect of mature, wise *people of God*, and the gradual but sometimes surprising process of restoration in the *timing of God*. We can learn a lot from the secular experts, but I want to be a little more graphic about various ways we try to cope with our pain.

Imagine that each of us is a house with a yard and a fence in a neighborhood. We have neighbors living next door, and there are people up and down the street and all over town. As we walk down the street, let's consider what we might see.

★ GOOD FENCES, STRONG GATE, GOOD NEIGHBOR

A few houses are well kept, with strong fences and working gates. A bell is hung next to the gate, and there's a sign that says, "Please ring. We'll be with you soon." The only way people can get in is to ring the bell, state their intentions, and be invited in. When visitors are finished with their business or their social visit, they leave through the gate. People enjoy visiting, and they're always glad to reciprocate and invite this person to their home.

This is a picture of an emotionally secure person with healthy boundaries and the choice to let people get close . . . or not. The fences are open and let people see the beauty of the garden and the handsome house, so many people are attracted as they walk by.

★ BROKEN HEART, BROKEN FENCE AND GATE

When we walk farther down the street, we pass by a house that hasn't been painted for years, the lawn and gardens are a mess, the fence is broken down in several places, and the gate is off its hinges. The sign on the remaining post says, "Take whatever you want. I can't stop you." The neighbors get only a few glimpses of the person who lives inside.

Some people are so beaten down that they don't have enough self-confidence to take care of themselves. They feel defeated, vulnerable, and threatened. Their defense is to just give up and let people walk over them. When someone asks for their opinion, they mumble, "I don't know. You decide." They don't have the strength to say "yes," and they don't have the courage to say "no." They have become passive, depressed, and helpless. They're deeply hurt, and they've given up on love and life.

★ HIGH WALLS AND A MACHINE GUN NEST

A house nearby doesn't have a nice picket fence; instead, it has concrete walls that are ten feet tall, and the metal gate is locked shut. No one can see the house, the garden, or the person who lives there...except when they look up and notice him manning the machine gun turret at the front corner of the lot! Any courageous people who try to speak to him are risking a burst of bullets. Most of the neighbors have learned it's best to cross the street and walk by on the other side.

Some people who have been deeply hurt react with defiance: "No one is ever going to hurt me again!" As long as no one bothers them, they can be pleasant, but if anyone takes one step too close, she gets blasted!

✱ MISPLACED ATTENTION

Down the street we see a strange sight. A person with a shattered gate and a dilapidated fence isn't at home. She's running around the neighborhood working on the garden of the person who feels helpless, and she paints the walls of the neighbor behind the machine gun. She's busy taking care of others, and she's neglecting her own home.

These are people we often honor as "so compassionate," "so helpful," and "so selfless," but their behavior is driven by the need to be needed, a compulsion to please to win acceptance, and the drive to be indispensable to others. They're so busy taking care of others that they don't have time (and don't want time) to examine their own lives and address their underlying fear, hurt, and anger.

Do you recognize anyone on this street? Do you see yourself? My purpose isn't to condemn any of the people who have broken fences or live behind high walls—they're doing the best they can to accomplish two goals: protect themselves from being hurt again and win at least some measure of approval. Of course, some lean more toward one of these goals than the other. I've seen these responses in people on staff teams, among friends, in families, and in myself.

THE CULTURE OF HIDING

We talk often about love, forgiveness, and grace, but many Christians are afraid to be honest about their flaws and fears. How can that be? I've seen it too many times—when Christians are bleeding, other believers are like piranha in the water. Instead of showing compassion, they quickly condemn. Instead of patiently listening to the person's problem, they form their judgment (almost always a negative judgment) right away. Instead of offering quiet consolation, they unleash the venom of gossip. Are these tendencies really worse in the Christian community? It sure seems that way to me. In the secular world, when a couple gets divorced, they keep their jobs, their reputations aren't too badly tarnished, and their friends are even closer (except for those who side with the ex). But quite often in the church, and especially with Christian leaders, failure has far greater consequences. The first thing to go is their reputations. They've fallen from being "the righteous" to become one of "the wicked." They lose many of their friends, and only the most loyal stick with them—and those friends are taking a great risk of being labeled "soft on sin." And of course, those in the ministry may lose more than their reputations; they may lose their livelihoods and their careers.

I'VE SEEN IT TOO MANY TIMES — WHEN CHRISTIANS ARE BLEEDING. OTHER BELIEVERS ARE LIKE PIRANHA IN THE WATER.

I'm certainly not suggesting we turn a blind eye to sin. Instead, I'm suggesting we develop a perspective that's more like Christ's. When Jesus and His disciples were invited to the home of Simon the Pharisee for dinner, the host watched in horror as a woman barged in. Her clothes indicated she was a prostitute, and she was well aware that she wasn't welcomed there. But something compelled her to come. We can guess that she had met Jesus on the street earlier that day, and His kindness and love had captured her heart. In Simon's dining room, she wept grateful tears, cleaning Jesus' feet with them and her long hair. She kissed His feet and poured expensive perfume on them. Simon was shocked and outraged.

How dare a woman of the street come into his home! And how dare Jesus let her perform this obvious demonstration of love!

> At that moment, Jesus asked Simon a piercing question: "Two people owed money to a certain moneylender. One owed him five hundred denarii, and the other fifty. Neither of them had the money to pay him back, so he forgave the debts of both. Now which of them will love him more?"

> Simon answered, "I supposed the one who had the bigger debt forgiven." Jesus affirmed that this was the right answer, and He pointed out the dramatic contrast between Simon and the woman:

> Then he turned toward the woman and said to Simon, "Do you see this woman? I came into your house. You did not give me any water for my feet, but she wet my feet with her tears and wiped them with her hair. You did not give me a kiss, but this woman, from the time I entered, has not stopped kissing my feet. You did not put oil on my head, but she has poured perfume on my feet. Therefore, I tell you, her many sins have been forgiven—as her great love has shown. But whoever has been forgiven little loves little." (Luke 7:36-47)

Was Jesus soft on sin? Some in our churches today would be on the side of Simon, demanding swift exclusion and severe judgment, but Jesus had another agenda, one of love and restoration.

Legalism and moralism are too common in our communities of faith. Legalism is the demand that we follow the Bible's commands to be acceptable to God, and moralism is a softer version of the same error—if we're nice enough, we'll be acceptable to God. But both are based on performance, not grace, so they necessarily result in comparison. We look around to see if others are performing better than we are, and we feel ashamed, or we're doing better than they are, and we look down our noses at them in pride. This isn't a safe environment for us to be honest about our deepest feelings and secrets!

It's fundamental human nature to default to the self-effort of legalism or moralism. God's amazing grace can be really hard to comprehend and even harder to fully accept for ourselves. One of our most important tasks as leaders is to present the grace of God compellingly and consistently so that people become convinced that God truly loves them. Grace alone creates the environment for hearts to be changed. In his commentary on Galatians, Martin Luther described the role of pastors and teachers: "Here I must take counsel of the gospel. I must harken to the gospel, which teaches me, not what I ought to do . . . but what Jesus Christ the Son of God has done for me . . . Most necessary it is, therefore, that we should know this article well, teach it to others . . . continually."[13] If I may paraphrase Luther: Whatever it takes, ask God to use you to help others comprehend and experience God's vivid, real, and life-changing grace.

At another level, some of us overpromise the benefits of the Christian life. To make it more attractive, we claim that becoming a Christian will make your marriage better, your kids more obedient, your body healthier, and your job more fulfilling. There certainly are benefits from our salvation, but we do people a grave disservice when we promise more than God intends to deliver. That sets them up for needing to lie when they experience anything less than total victory all day every day. Unrealistic expectations inevitably have destructive consequences.

The culture of hiding and posing may seem completely normal to us, but it contributes to increased isolation, more entrenched shame, and the perception that other people don't have the level of problems we have. Because the love of God gives us security and affection, we should be the most honest and open people on the planet, but instead, we often live behind walls to keep our secrets. Image management, not authenticity, is the way most of us live.

Gossip poisons the church's culture. When we've heard people talk about others, and when we've participated in "sharing our concerns," we realize not a shred of information about us is safe if it gets out. Knowledge is power, and when someone knows something about us that is less than flattering, we lose the power to control our narrative. People can (and will) say virtually anything about us that makes them look like "people in the know."

> IF I MAY PARAPHRASE LUTHER: WHATEVER IT TAKES, ASK GOD TO USE YOU TO HELP OTHERS COMPREHEND AND EXPERIENCE GOD'S VIVID, REAL, AND LIFE-CHANGING GRACE.

LIVING COLOR

Many years ago, the movie *Pleasantville* came out. The storyline is that a young man, David, spends a lot of time watching a black-and-white 50s sitcom called *Pleasantville*, about the bland and always-pleasant lives of the Parker family. One day David and his sister Jennifer fight over the remote control and break it, so their mother calls a television repairman. When he arrives, he gives them another remote, and when they use it, David and Jennifer magically find themselves in the Parkers' living room—back in time, and in black and white. They begin to introduce people in the town to new adventures, and as the people respond, they become colorized. As more and more people are transformed from black-and-white to color, the city's leaders feel threatened and institute a ban on "colored" people. A riot eventually erupts, and David and a friend are put on trial. They are exonerated, and more of the town becomes saturated with living color. In the end, David returns to the real world, but Jennifer chooses to stay in the comfort and blandness of Pleasantville.[14]

This is, I believe, an analogy of many church communities. Life's difficult questions are often met with religion's too quick and too easy answers. We live a bland, superficially happy but colorless existence. When someone comes along to inject a new reality into us, a deeper, more honest way to live, some people thrive but others feel threatened. The question in the movie and in our churches is the same: Who will win in the trial—those who advocate the color of authenticity or those who feel more comfortable living in a lifeless black-and-white world?

When we hide to protect our reputations, we're always playing defense. But when we find at least one person who will listen to our stories, we tap into enormous resources of spiritual power. We learn to build strong fences and a sound gate so we can choose who to let in and who to exclude. Before we worry about trying to fix other people, we commit to first take care of what's inside the fence: *our* emotions, desires, purpose, and choices. Then, as strong, secure, confident people, we can engage with others in the neighborhood, even offering the guy manning the machine gun a chance to talk if he wants to.

Some of us need to rebuild our fences, reinforce our gates, and do a lot of work on our houses and yards. Others need to begin taking down their concrete walls, block by block, so they can initiate real relationships. And some need to stay home and mind their own business for a while! When we find the courage of a lion to speak the truth to at least one person, we may eventually discover that the things that seemed like kryptonite are really a superpower. We'll be wiser, stronger, more compassionate than ever before, and we'll have something incredibly valuable to offer others: our true selves.

A few years ago, I was at a national conference. On the first morning, I found a seat beside another pastor. I said, "Hi, my name is Jonathan."

He sat up and excitedly told me, "My name is Phil, and our church gave a million dollars to missions last year!"

I wondered why in the world that would be his lead-in to introduce himself. I'm sure he had figured this would be his most impressive opening. In one way, it was. At the time, our church's entire budget wasn't a million dollars. But rather than feel offended, I decided to celebrate him instead. After all, I was pretty sure he'd be the most fun guy at any party he attended, and I didn't want to miss out on the thrill. I said, "That's amazing! Just think about all the people around the world who now know Jesus because of your church's generosity. What a great legacy play!"

That wasn't the reaction he anticipated. His shoulders dropped, and the look in his eyes softened. His comment had been the opening salvo in his anticipated comparison battle of our churches, but when I didn't fight back, he was totally disarmed. Thirty seconds later, he launched into telling me about the myriad of frustrations he'd experienced as the pastor of his church. After unburdening his heart, he asked, "Jonathan, would you pray for me?"

I said, "I'll be glad to."

When I didn't bite on his bid to begin the comparison game, he relaxed, felt safe, and was thoroughly himself.

We often tell people, "God loves you and has a wonderful plan for your life," and that's true, but He also has a wonderful plan for your past. He wants to redeem every part of it. Do you want a superpower? Find a trustworthy person to talk to, and find the courage to take one more step toward vulnerability. Tell your story, and then tell it again with more details, and then tell it again. That's how it happens. At least with a trusted friend (or counselor or mentor), you don't have to play the comparison game any longer, and you don't have to be an expert in image management. Like the pastor I met at the conference, you can be yourself, and like Miss Molly told me, "You can be the person God wants you to be."

The "lions" I walk with hear my story with patience and kindness, and they hear it again. They're helping me become the person God wants me to be.

consider
THIS

1

Can you relate to any parts of my story? If you can, describe the connection. If not, I'm sure you know someone who has had an experience somewhat similar to mine. How has abuse or abandonment affected that person?

....

....

....

....

....

....

2

What difference does it mean to have someone like Miss Molly in our lives?

....

....

....

....

....

....

....

....

3

Which of the houses
in the neighborhood
vignettes do you
relate to? Do you also
recognize other people
in the analogies?
Explain your answers.

....
....
....
....
....
....
....
....
....

4

Why should the church
be the safest place
on earth, and in what
ways is it unsafe?

....
....
....
....
....
....
....
....
....
....

5

At this point in the book, what's your perception of the cost and the benefit of finding one person who will invite you to be vulnerable?

....

....

....

....

....

....

....

....

....

....

....

....

....

....

....

....

....

....

....

....

WHEN PEOPLE TALK.
LISTEN
COMPLETELY.
MOST PEOPLE
NEVER LISTEN.

— ERNEST HEMINGWAY —

you
are
loved.

WOMEN'S CONFERENCE
REZ CHURCH
OCTOBER 2020

CHAPTER THREE

LISTENER

We often hear the message, "You have a God-given calling only you can fulfill." That's true, but it's not the whole story. God does indeed give us individual assignments, but that doesn't necessarily mean He holds us solely responsible for getting the job done. Throughout our lives, and particularly in crucial moments, God calls others to help us fulfill our calling. To modify the old credit card commercial, "Don't leave home without them." Don't do life alone. Don't do leadership alone. Don't do ministry alone.

Jesus, the incarnate Son of God, had a unique calling. We quote John 3:16, we remember that He said He came "to seek and to save the lost," and we read about the many instances when He told the disciples He had come to redeem people from sin. He connected His calling to the prophesies in the Old Testament when He told them, "We are going up to Jerusalem, and everything that is written by the prophets about the Son of Man will be fulfilled. He will be delivered over to the Gentiles. They will mock him, insult him and spit on him; they will flog him and kill him. On the third day he will rise again" (Luke 18:31-33).

After His arrest, kangaroo court trial, and condemnation, the next morning Jesus was taken to Pilate, who offered the crowd a choice. It was his custom

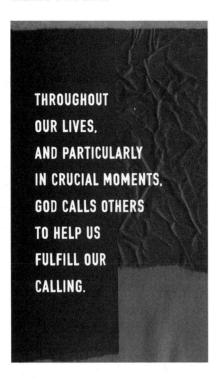

THROUGHOUT OUR LIVES, AND PARTICULARLY IN CRUCIAL MOMENTS, GOD CALLS OTHERS TO HELP US FULFILL OUR CALLING.

to release a prisoner at Passover, and he offered them either Jesus or Barabbas, who had committed murder and insurrection—the very crimes crucifixion was designed to punish. The crowd chose to release Barabbas. (In an ironic twist, *Barabbas* means "son of the father." The real Son of the Father gave His life in place of the "son of the father.")

Jesus was brutally whipped, a process that ripped the flesh off the prisoner's back. Then, He was led to Golgotha to die. On the way, He was ordered to carry His own cross, but He had been beaten so badly and lost so much blood that He couldn't carry it all the way. Matthew puts us at the scene: "As they were going out, they met a man from Cyrene, named Simon, and they forced him to carry the cross" (Matthew 27:32). Only hours before, He had told Peter, "Where I am going, you cannot follow Me now, but you will follow later" (John 13:36). He was saying that His calling was something only He could accomplish, but on the way to pay the penalty for the sins of the world, He needed help.

CARRYING BURDENS

Does this apply to us? Yes, in spades! Sometimes we need someone to come alongside and carry our burden for us, and other times we're in Simon's shoes and carry the cross of a friend. Paul explained the breadth of this responsibility and privilege in his letter to the Galatians. That church was a messed-up bunch. They had responded to Paul's preaching years before, but after he left, some Jewish leaders came to town and taught the Gentiles that they had to become Jewish before they could become Christians—in other words, they had to fulfill the law before they could follow Jesus. The leaders were loading the Gentiles with a burden even they had been unable to carry! In his letter, Paul corrected their thinking about the role of the law and the message of grace, and then he pleaded with them, "Brothers and sisters, if someone is caught in a sin, you who live by the Spirit should restore that person gently. But watch yourselves, or you also may be tempted. Carry each other's burdens, and in this way you will fulfill the law of Christ" (Galatians 6:1-2).

What are the burdens people can't carry on their own? They may include a past trauma, an addiction, a specific sin, a pattern of sin, a character flaw, crushing debt, a failing marriage, wayward kids, or anything else that weighs them down . . . and weighs us down. How do we bear them? Perhaps in many ways, but it all starts with listening. In fact, the name *Simon* means "listener." When Jesus couldn't carry His burden, a listener came to help Him. That's what we need, too, and that's our role in others' lives.

MEDICATORS

Matthew gives us another look into the events surrounding the crucifixion: "They came to a place called Golgotha (which means 'the place of the skull'). There they offered Jesus wine to drink, mixed with gall; but after tasting it, he refused to drink it" (Matthew 27:33-34). Crucifixion was an excruciating way to die. The nails tore at ligaments and tendons in the most sensitive parts of the body. It often took days for people to finally succumb to the pain, blood loss, and asphyxiation because their chests were immobile. To ease the suffering, the executioners offered the convicted person a painkiller: "wine . . . mixed with gall." Jesus shared His burden with a friend, Simon, but He refused a medication to deaden the pain.

When we think of "addiction" and "medicating our pain," we naturally envision certain drugs and perhaps alcohol, but we can easily identify other ways we try to numb our emotional pain. Certainly, we may use substances, but we also use behaviors like vegging out in front of the television, being absorbed in social media, making sure we're never alone for long, diversionary shopping, workaholism, pornography, over- or under-eating, sleeping too much, obsessively controlling people and events, and many other diversions. If our lives are empty and dull, we find something to make us excited, like cheering for our favorite team, or something that inflames our anger, like the fury in much of our political dialogue. Some of these behaviors give us a momentary thrill, which boosts levels of brain chemicals and make us feel better, but others simply occupy our thoughts so we don't have to feel or think about the problems in our lives. We unconsciously create a lifestyle that prevents us from feeling too deeply, thinking too accurately, and having to deal with the buried reality of our fear, hurt, anger, and shame.

A number of studies show that the urge to medicate emotional pain is heightened when we're isolated.[15] Loneliness has two negative effects: it increases stress and reduces support and accountability. We can feel isolated in a crowd when we don't have at least one person who knows us deeply and loves us truly. There's an old saying, "You're only as sick as your secrets." "Sick" isn't limited to physiological illness; it describes emotional and psychological problems, too.

But the opposite is also true: participating in a vibrant community significantly reduces the compulsion to self-medicate through any means, chemical or behavioral. Psychiatrist Lloyd I. Sederer updated a study conducted in the 1970s. Rats were isolated in a cage and given two options: water, or a liquid laced with heroin or cocaine. The lonely rats drank the laced liquid until they died from overdoses. Then the scientists put another group in "rat parks," where they were free to socialize. When they were given the same choice, "they remarkably preferred the plain water. . . . A social community beat the power of drugs." Sederer makes the application to the practice of psychiatry (and by extension, any other healing community):

> Humans, not just rats, need to be part of a community, encouraged to relate and experience the support of others. This is about as basic a psychological truth as exists, yet does it find application in clinicians' offices?
>
> How many of us, during clinical encounters with patients, focus on their families, their social communities, their sources of human contact and support? . . .
>
> Mother Theresa [*sic*], not someone often quoted in medical journals, said, "If you want to change the world, go home and love your family." I think the Beatles said the same thing. And when we see people and families who are keeping their emotional heads above the often roiling waters of everyday life, who are not compulsively imbibing on drug-laced concoctions, or pathologically gambling or playing video games and the like, we will see that they lead their lives in the light of relationships, in human parks, not alone.[16]

We can thrive only when we feel loved and accepted. But that statement surfaces the underlying problem: most of us aren't vulnerable enough, or with the right people, to feel known and loved. Keeping our secrets seems safer, but like the lonely rats, our compulsions and addictions will kill us. Connection is the opposite of addiction . . . and it's the antidote.

CHOOSE YOUR LISTENER WISELY

Who is qualified to be your Simon—someone you can count on to provide strength and support to lighten a heavy burden? Start by considering a counselor, a coach, a friend, an aunt or uncle, a parent, a mentor, or your spouse. Then, look for two primary qualifications, both of which are requirements: very simply, is the person *willing* and *able*? Some people are willing, but they aren't competent or emotionally healthy enough to help us, and some are able, but they're either not available or not interested. A friend on our staff team thought about these qualities and concluded, "I never want to waste my vulnerability." That's good advice.

We naturally see Judas, the disciple who betrayed Jesus, as a traitor, but we seldom look at a vulnerable moment that happened later that night. The chief priests had paid him to turn on Jesus, but later, he had a change of heart: "When Judas, who had betrayed him, saw that Jesus was condemned, he was seized with remorse and returned the thirty pieces of silver to the chief priests and the elders. 'I have sinned,' he said, 'for I have betrayed innocent blood.'"

Judas was doing exactly what I'm suggesting in this chapter: confessing his sin to someone who should have been glad to hear it. How did the priests respond? "What is that to us?" they replied. "That's your responsibility."

Matthew tells us the result: "So Judas threw the money into the temple and left. Then he went away and hanged himself" (Matthew 27:3-5).

The priests weren't willing to be listeners for Judas. In *Indiana Jones and the Last Crusade*, when the bad guy chose the wrong chalice and was horribly melted in judgment, the attending knight said simply, "He chose poorly." And Judas chose poorly. It can happen to any of us. We need at least some assurance that the people we want to confide in are willing to be good listeners.

> CONNECTION IS THE OPPOSITE OF ADDICTION... AND IT'S THE ANTIDOTE.

Others are willing but not able to listen. They don't have the position or the skill to help those in need. In one of the most amazing scenes in the life of David, he was being chased by King Saul and his army. For a second time, David had an opportunity to kill Saul, but instead, he only took a spear and a jug of water near Saul's head as he slept. David stood on a nearby hill and called out to Saul and his army, revealing how vulnerable they had been. The king realized (for the moment) that his pursuit of David was in vain. Saul called back, "I have sinned. Come back, David my son. Because you considered my life precious today, I will not try to harm you again. Surely I have acted like a fool and have been terribly wrong" (1 Samuel 26:21).

David chose not to be Saul's confidante. He was in a weak position, running for his life. It's good that Saul admitted his fault to David, but the young man wasn't in a position where he could come alongside and help his adversary deal with his sin. Was David hardhearted for not playing the role of a trusted friend? No, he was wise. Only a few verses later, Saul was after him again. It would have been foolish for David to trust him. Look for these qualities in the person you choose to carry your burden, and develop them in your life. Look for someone who . . .

* IS GENTLE ⟶ KIND AND TENDERHEARTED

* IS DISCREET ⟶ HAS NO HISTORY OF GOSSIP

* HAS EARNED YOUR TRUST ⟶ YOU'VE SEEN THEIR INTEGRITY

* HAS A TRACK RECORD OF RESTORING OTHERS
   ↳ YOU AREN'T THE PERSON'S TEST CASE

* HAS BLIND SPOTS THAT ARE DIFFERENT FROM YOURS
   ↳ THEY SEE WHAT YOU DON'T

* LOVES YOU BUT ISN'T IMPRESSED WITH YOU → YOU AREN'T ON A PEDESTAL

* ISN'T SHAKEN BY YOUR CRISIS
   ↳ HAS BEEN AROUND THE BLOCK A FEW TIMES

* CHALLENGES YOU TO BE BETTER ⟶ COMFORTS AND STRETCHES YOU

* SAYS, WITH KINDNESS, WHAT YOU DON'T WANT TO HEAR
   ↳ SPEAKS THE TRUTH IN LOVE

* MOVES YOU TOWARD GREATER FREEDOM AND HEALING
   ↳ HAS A GENUINELY POSITIVE IMPACT.

Finding someone who isn't shocked by your honesty is really important. I heard a story about two Catholic priests, a mentor and one in training. The older man wanted to hear how the young priest heard parishioners' confessions, so the two of them sat together on one side of the screen listening to people who had come to bear their souls. After the last one, they walked out of the booth, and the young priest asked, "How did I do?" The older man responded, "Well, you did pretty well, but there's one thing I need to point out."

"What's that?" the eager young priest asked.

"When people confess their sins, maybe you should stop saying, 'GOLLEEEE!'"

BUT WHO?

Like you, I've heard horror stories of people who took a step to be open with someone, and it was a disaster. A pastor found the courage to tell his mentor about his recurring problem with pornography. He expected understanding, support, and confidentiality, but his mentor wrote a letter to the pastor's board detailing the behavior and recommending they put him on an "indefinite leave of absence." Should he have been disqualified for his role as a pastor? In my view, we shouldn't punish people for seeking help. Certainly, some sins disqualify people from leadership positions, but in many cases, healing and restoration can happen in the context of continued service.

In a similar situation, a staff member told his pastor about his pornography and masturbation. The pastor listened intently, and then he pronounced, "You need to tell your wife."

The man explained, "My wife told me years ago that if I ever have a problem with porn, she doesn't want to know. She wants me to deal with it and get help, but not to tell her about it."

"She really doesn't mean that," the pastor told him. "You need to tell her, and you need to tell her today."

The staff member went home and told his wife about his problem. She was predictably horrified. She packed up the kids and left to spend several days with her parents. Of course, they asked why she had come so unexpectedly, and she told them.

Her husband was devastated. He felt ashamed, betrayed, and exposed. The pastor tried to tell him he had done the right thing, but his words fell flat. The pastor then called me and asked, "Jonathan, what did I do wrong?"

"Well," I explained, "for starters, you could have gotten him the help he needed while respecting his wife's wishes. He planned to do exactly what his wife wanted him to do, but you didn't let him. It's not your role to challenge his wife's clearly expressed desire."

Couples may have very different expectations. One may reasonably want everything to be out in the open, but another may, like the wife in this story, just as reasonably want to set some limits on vulnerability. There's no right or wrong . . . as long as they've communicated their wishes very clearly.

Miss Molly was the first resource for me, but she wasn't the last. I've asked a number of people to be confidantes—a counselor and a few dear friends who "are closer than a brother." In a talk on this topic, Pastor and author Tim Keller identifies four marks of true friendship: **constancy, carefulness, candor, and council.**

★ CONSTANCY

"A friend loves at all times" (Proverbs 17:17). This doesn't mean the friend is always present; it means a friend is present in all kinds of times—good and bad, boring and thrilling.

★ CAREFULNESS

A friend handles our emotions with tenderness. He weeps when we weep and rejoices when we rejoice.

★ CANDOR

A friend doesn't let us walk down the wrong road very far. When he needs to say something hard to us, it's with a wonderful blend of kindness and honesty. "Better is open rebuke than hidden love. Wounds from a friend can be trusted, but an enemy multiplies kisses" (Proverbs 27:5-6). A true friend loves enough to wound us when it's necessary.

★ COUNCIL

Friends give advice sparingly, but in a timely and appropriate way, knowing us well enough to articulate it so we're able to hear it instead of rejecting the input.

Keller points to two reasons it's hard to find friends like this: first, we're a mobile culture, and people move away faster than we can replace these deep connections, and second, we're not the kind of people who attract or gravitate to people who are mature, wise, honest, and strong. They seem like threats to us! [17]

POWER DIFFERENTIALS

A pastor who heard me speak about the power of honest relationships saw a potential flaw in my thinking. He asked, "Jonathan, you talk about having vulnerable relationships with people on your staff team, but you're their boss. Isn't that a dual relationship? How can they feel free to be completely honest when you hold power over them?"

It's a great question, one that I've thought a lot about. And there are others. You may be asking:

* WHAT IF SOMEONE TELLS ME SOMETHING REALLY, REALLY BAD, AND EVEN DANGEROUS?

* HOW CAN I FORCE MY TEAM TO BE MORE OPEN?

* HOW SHOULD I RESPOND IF MY LEADER TRIES TO FORCE ME TO BE OPEN?

* WHERE'S THE LINE OF WHEN SOMEONE IS FIRED AND WHEN SHE IS RESTORED?

* WHEN IS A PROBLEM TOO BIG, TOO DEEP, TOO COMPLEX FOR THE LEADER TO HANDLE?

* WHAT'S THE BALANCE (IF THERE IS ONE) OF GIVING GRACE AND HOLDING PEOPLE ACCOUNTABLE?

* HOW MUCH TIME SHOULD WE GIVE PEOPLE TO CHANGE AND GROW?

Some leaders are shepherds, caring for the people under them, while others see their roles primarily as CEOs whose purpose is to stimulate excellent performance and achieve corporate goals. The two approaches don't have to be mutually exclusive. However, when leaders become too driven and goal-oriented to create a positive, healthy environment, they risk creating a toxic culture of fear, gossip, sniping, or apathy.

Let me share the guardrails I've communicated to our team to help them have confidence in the process and determine how much to share, to whom, how, and when. In fact, these are the guidelines I recommend to any leader and group:

- Each state has mandatory reporting requirements, including any threat of homicide or suicide, or incidents of sexual abuse, physical abuse, child abuse or neglect, or elder abuse or neglect. In addition, I'm required to report any fire-able offenses to our board. People need to know that you don't have an option to keep such things confidential.

- Limit vulnerability to the level of trust the leader has earned. Be cautious if the leader feels threatened by anyone's honesty, is superficial about his own problems, or weaponizes anyone's vulnerability by using it against them.

- Limit sharing in group settings to people telling their stories. Anything deeper should be shared privately at the person's discretion, not the leader's.

- Limit sharing if anyone on the team isn't trustworthy. The leader may be wonderfully honest and supportive, but it only takes one gossip to ruin relationships.

- In some cases, problems are deeper than what the leader can handle, so appropriate referrals to counselors or physicians should be made.

- Similarly, professional intervention may be necessary in cases of addiction, adultery, or other destructive behavior. You may already have a strong relationship with a counselor skilled in this approach, but if not, find one. It's not wise to attempt this on your own unless you have a lot of experience because the stakes are too high.

Understandably, leaders ask me how I handle sticky situations when people share a struggle that might disqualify them from their current roles. I lean hard toward the hope of restoration, but I'm not naïve. I get feedback from the professional, not just the staff member, and I often eliminate or reduce the responsibilities of the person. I've seen leaders react and immediately fire the person, but I suspect this happens, at least some of the time, to protect the leader's image. I've also witnessed leaders go to the other extreme and refuse to deal with very sticky problems. For them, a quick apology was enough, and life goes on . . . without resolving the issue in any substantive way. These leaders often claim they're "giving grace" to the offender. But that's not grace; that's denial.

MY ROLE

I see my role as a supportive friend and advocate. I care for the people on our team, and I invite them to tell me as much or as little as they want. I never push. It's always up to them to determine what and how much to share. (You'll read this several times in this book because it's crucial.) I want to hold people accountable, but never in a punitive way. Most often, accountability sounds like, "The last time we talked, you said you wanted to do this or that. How's it going?" I want them to know that I'll listen far more than I'll advise, and I'll care far more than I'll challenge.

As much as I'm an advocate for creating environments of vulnerability and support, I'm very uncomfortable when I hear stories of leaders who press their people to be more open. It needs to be an invitation, not a demand. It must flow from a relationship of trust, not coercion.

Should we leave people in their roles as they get help? Obviously, it depends on the nature of the problem, but my general principle is that it's far better for most people to be honest, come into the light, and actively pursue repentance, healing, and growth in their current roles than to be sidelined (and probably shamed) by taking them out of their roles as they get the help they need. My questions in these situations are simple:

★ WILL REMAINING IN THE ROLE HURT OR HELP OTHER PEOPLE?

★ WILL REMAINING IN THE ROLE SOMEHOW HINDER THE PERSON'S HEALING AND GROWTH?

I realize I often don't have the expertise to answer these questions myself, so I ask some highly gifted, experienced people to give me their input. They know far more than I do about what it takes to overcome the ravages of substance abuse, depression, adultery, and various types of abuse, which often leave the person with a measure of PTSD.

Far too many church leaders gravitate toward simplistic solutions to complex problems. We want to have "the answers," and we live in a culture

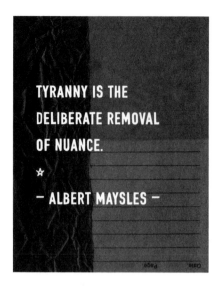

TYRANNY IS THE
DELIBERATE REMOVAL
OF NUANCE.

★

— ALBERT MAYSLES —

that provides everything instantly. But we need to slow down, ask more questions, listen more carefully, and craft our response. Documentary filmmaker Albert Maysles observed, "Tyranny is the deliberate removal of nuance."

Today, we're seeing a marked increase in anxiety and depression among leaders and their teams. In an article in *Christianity Today*, Stephanie Dyrness Lobdell asserts:

Recent statistics demonstrate that clergy are prone to high levels of stress and burnout, factors that contribute to the likelihood of depressive episodes. A challenging job combined with certain biological features in the brain can result in major depressive disorder in clergy, regardless of race, age, or theological tradition.

At the same time, the church has often been silent, or at least guarded, on depression—not for lack of caring, but for lack of understanding. Lay Christians and church leaders struggle with the apparent cognitive dissonance between depression and the Christian life. "If Jesus has achieved the victory, why am I so sad? If God reigns and is working to redeem creation, why am I mired in hopelessness and exhaustion before the day begins?" Those are the questions we may ask ourselves. . . .

While the church hasn't intended to wound those who suffer from depression, a lack of understanding has often done that. Thankfully, as medical science continues to learn more about the brain and how to effectively treat conditions like depression, misconceptions surrounding depression are being dismantled. [18]

We need to be much more aware of the quite varied symptoms of depression—and not be surprised when we see them in ourselves and in the people around us. A study by Duke University found that clergy members experience depression at twice the rate as the general population.[19]

My approach to anyone on our team who's struggling isn't a blanket, one-size-fits-all approach. Honoring their honesty by keeping them in their current role is my preferred process unless it's clear the person is disqualified. If the person needs to step away from his responsibilities for a while, my hope is that the break will provide the necessary restorative process so he or she can come back into a meaningful role—probably not soon, but someday. This approach requires, as you can tell, a lot of wisdom, patience, grace, and brutal honesty. Vulnerability has its costs, but also its rewards. I'd much rather our team be genuinely healthy than be perceived as scandal-free.

Lions listen.

A CALCULATED CHOICE

I understand the desire of pastors and other leaders to protect their organizations and their own reputations by getting rid of people with delicate or disturbing problems, or acting like those problems don't exist. But what if we were secure

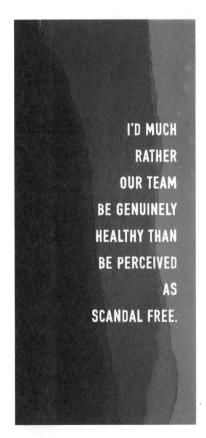

I'D MUCH RATHER OUR TEAM BE GENUINELY HEALTHY THAN BE PERCEIVED AS SCANDAL FREE.

enough in ourselves and confident enough in God building His church that we loved people like Jesus loved the ones around Him? Over and over again, He risked His reputation to reach out and love people—sick people, lame people, poor people, lepers, women, children, adulterers, tax collectors, prostitutes, and thieves, to name a few. All of those were considered second-class in their society, but Jesus didn't follow the religious norms. He braved the scorn of the self-righteous to heal the hearts of the marginalized.

The same choice is in our hands.

1

Do you have a Simon in your life? In whose life are you a good "listener"?

....

....

....

....

....

....

....

2

What are some "medicators" used by people you know? Which one(s) have you used? What has been the benefit, and what's the downside of using them?

....

....

....

....

....

....

....

3

What are some signs someone is willing to sit with you, invite you to be vulnerable, and really listen? What are some signs a person is able to be a listener?

....
....
....
....
....
....
....
....
....
....

4

Is your spouse comfortable being the willing and able listener for you? Explain your answer.

....
....
....
....
....
....
....
....
....
....

5

Which of the guardrails in this chapter seem most important to you? Which ones do you need to explore more carefully?

....

....

....

....

....

....

....

....

....

6

At this point, after reading and reflecting on the benefits and limitations of vulnerability, what is your calculated choice about whether to wade into the mess of people's lives?

....

....

....

....

....

....

....

....

....

DARKNESS

CANNOT

DRIVE OUT

DARKNESS,

ONLY

LIGHT

CAN DO THAT.

—

MARTIN
LUTHER KING, JR.

—

CHAPTER FOUR

THE POWER OF LIGHT

Not long after Amy and I were married, I served as the worship pastor at a church in Lake Providence, Louisiana. We met in a corrugated metal building with a gravel parking lot. One Sunday morning, long before the service was to start, I was sitting alone in the lobby where I could see through the glass walls and double doors. A couple of enormous, decorative potted plants flanked the doors. I was on the phone (a landline, if you can remember that far back) talking to Amy. Suddenly, a car sped around the corner, came in hot, slid on the gravel, and skidded to a stop right in front of the door. It was a couple on my worship team, Jamie and Michelle. As soon as Jamie turned off the engine, I could hear them arguing—all the way from the front seat of their car, past the giant plants, and through the glass walls and doors. They were going at it, and it looked like the fight was about to escalate from stun to *kill!*

Jamie got out first, but he was still barking at Michelle after the door closed. She got out with daggers in her eyes, snarling back at him. Jamie walked toward the door. I wanted to run, but I was stuck because I was tethered by the phone cord. He opened the door, but he didn't see me. He walked in a couple of steps, turned to Michelle, stuck his tongue out and let out a "Thbbbllllpppbbbppptttt!"

With his tongue still out, he turned and saw me. I didn't say a word, mostly because I was stunned into silence. Instantly, he reeled his tongue back in, straightened up, turned, smiled at Michelle, and said sweetly, "Let's go to church, honey."

What was the difference between Jamie acting like a three-year-old and acting like a mature, loving husband? Did he have a radical heart change the instant he saw me? I wish, but I'm pretty sure that's not what happened. He changed because he realized I was looking at him. He had walked into the light of my vision. (And by the way, he loves this story!)

We can't will ourselves (or another person) to emotional health. It doesn't work that way. A vital step is to bring what was hidden into sight, what was in darkness into the light.

INTO THE LIGHT

The power of light is one of the most common themes in the Bible. In a dark room, we bump into things and we get confused about which way to go, but when a light comes on, we can see how to navigate the furniture. In John's first letter, in the very first chapter, he describes the necessity of light for believers:

> This is the message we have heard from him and declare to you: God is light; in him there is no darkness at all. If we claim to have fellowship with him and yet walk in the darkness, we lie and do not live out the truth. But if we walk in the light, as he is in the light, we have fellowship with one another, and the blood of Jesus, his Son, purifies us from all sin.

> If we claim to be without sin, we deceive ourselves and the truth is not in us. If we confess our sins, he is faithful and just and will forgive us our sins and purify us from all unrighteousness. If we claim we have not sinned, we make him out to be a liar and his word is not in us. (1 John 1:5-10)

John confirms what we've said about hiding, posing, and medicating. He contrasts a person who "walks in darkness" (who isn't honest about his sins, his flaws, and his need for God's healing, forgiving touch) with one who "walks in the light" and experiences the healing and forgiveness we long for. When we can't or won't admit our flaws, we also try to pull the wool over others' eyes. But if we're humble enough and brave enough to agree with God about our sins, we experience His presence, His power, and His cleansing.

Light is threatening to those who want to stay in darkness, but it's liberating for those who choose to live in the truth—the truth about God, the truth about their past and present, the truth about other people, and the truth about all the events in their lives.

These days many of us aren't very good at confession. We don't want to admit we need it, even as we're eager to point out others' faults. Maybe we've seen others get blasted for being honest, but more likely, we're like Adam and Eve, very well aware of our shame and wanting to keep it hidden at all costs.

Confession doesn't *earn* God's forgiveness; we're already completely forgiven through the blood of Jesus. Instead, confession enables us to experience

> **"WE CAN'T WILL OURSELVES (OR ANOTHER PERSON) TO EMOTIONAL HEALTH.**

the forgiveness God has already given us. Some of us who are Protestants look down our noses at the Catholic practice of confessing to a priest, but there's power in verbalizing our sins to another person—a safe person, but another person nonetheless. James, the half-brother of Jesus, encouraged us, "Therefore confess your sins to each other and pray for each other so that you may be healed. The prayer of a righteous person is powerful and effective" (James 5:16). When we're vulnerable with a safe person, our prayers become more real, fellowship becomes more supportive, and we can finally relax and breathe.

Many people claim they can walk with God without going to church or being involved in strong relationships with people. I beg to disagree. Throughout the Bible, we see faith in God planted, built, and strengthened through "iron sharpening iron" relationships—and without them, faith erodes. Even Jesus, the most self-sufficient person who ever lived, regularly took Peter, James, and John with Him to special places of ministry. In the Garden of Gethsemane, when He looked into the abyss of hell and began to feel the crushing weight of the sins of all mankind, He was disappointed when they didn't stay awake to pray with Him. John wrote in his first letter, "Whoever claims to love God yet hates a brother or sister is a liar. For whoever does not love their brother and sister, whom they have seen, cannot love God, whom they have not seen. And he has given us this command: Anyone who loves God must also love their brother and sister" (1 John 4:20-21). That night in the Garden, Peter, James, and John failed to love their brother.

Virtually every spiritual blessing is communicated and ratified in relationships with others. How do we know God loves us? It's when we feel unlovable and someone reaches out to bring us close. How do we know God forgives us? Because when we confess our sins to another believer and see the grace on that person's face, we sense God's forgiveness, too. How do we know God accepts us? It happens when we've blown it but another person still sees us as valuable.

Do you think I'm reading too much into this? Thanks for asking, but I don't think so. The heart of God and the heart of believers shouldn't be separate. They're woven seamlessly together. Look at these passages:

> We can express God's love to others only to the extent we experience His love, but when we genuinely encounter the love of God, we'll be eager for others to share the experience. "This is love: not that we loved God, but that he loved us and sent his Son as an atoning sacrifice for our sins. Dear friends, since God so loved us, we also ought to love one another" (1 John 4:10-11).

> We forgive others out of the deep well of our experience of God's forgiveness. "Get rid of all bitterness, rage and anger, brawling and slander, along with every form of malice. Be kind and compassionate to one another, forgiving each other, just as in Christ God forgave you" (Ephesians 4:31-32).

> And we accept people who are different, who have nothing to offer us, and who "aren't our kind," when we realize Jesus has accepted us when we sure weren't His kind. "Accept one another, then, just as Christ accepted you, in order to bring praise to God" (Romans 15:7).

The incomparable light of God's love, forgiveness, and acceptance gives us the courage to be honest when we feel unlovable, ashamed, and discarded. We then can share this light with the people around us who so desperately need it—and they can share it with us when we feel deeply discouraged. That's how the family of God should operate. That's how we get into the light and stay in the light.

I've had quite a number of moments when I've been surprised by the light of God's presence and power. The first was the day in Miss Molly's home office when I was desperate to tell someone about how my father had been treating me. When I brought the abuse into the light by speaking the truth, a floodgate of understanding, love, and acceptance opened for me. I'm convinced her response to me that day was how Jesus would have responded. Sometimes I tell people, "You look good! I see Jesus on you." And that's what I saw in Miss Molly . . . I saw Jesus in her—loving, listening without judging, protecting, and affirming me.

I've also experienced times when people who love me have spoken hard truth to me. Mentors, counselors, friends, and Amy have shined the light on areas of my life that had been in darkness far too long, and I'm a different person today because they loved me enough to speak up.

> **THE FATHER OF LIGHT DOESN'T WANT US TO USE OUR RELATIONSHIP WITH HIM AS PRETENSE TO STAY IN DARKNESS.**

Why do we confess our faults to each other? Because the Father of light doesn't want us to use our relationship with Him as pretense to stay in darkness. When we gloss over our sins by claiming "quick forgiveness," that's a form of denial, and it prevents us from being completely honest about our sins and experiencing God's love and forgiveness at the deepest level.

LIGHT AS A HEALER

Psychologists have identified one type of depression as "seasonal affective disorder." Those who suffer from it usually live in areas of the country where sunlight is limited, especially in late fall through early spring. Lower levels of light result in a range of symptoms that are common to many types of depression, including mood changes, fatigue, changes in sleep patterns and eating, withdrawal from people and pleasure, and random aches and pains. People are affected because the level of serotonin, a vital brain chemical that contributes to the feeling of happiness and well-being, drops below effective levels.[20]

I see many of the same symptoms in people who aren't walking in God's light! We can be very creative in our commitment to stay in darkness. Here are some things people have told me:

"I talk to God about my problems. It's nobody else's business."

"God and I have a deal: If God will get me out of the jam this time, I promise I'll never do it again."

"It's not that bad."

"I'm sure it'll get better."

"It's not really my fault."

Like a person suffering from seasonal affective disorder, the primary solution is more light. Light can do what nothing else can. In trauma care, medical professionals sometimes expose wounds to light and air. Spiritually and emotionally, light promotes healing, lifts spirits, provides clarity of direction, generates growth, and brings credibility. Time doesn't heal all things . . . unless the person walks in the light over that time. The light of truth illumines resources we didn't see when we were in darkness.

The psalmist wrote, "Your word is a lamp for my feet, a light on my path" (Psalm 119:105). Truth in all its forms—the truth of God's Word, the truth about ourselves, and the truth of how God wants to transform us—gives us courage for today and hope for tomorrow.

Actually, when we walk in the light with trusted people, accountability takes on a different hue. We often think of "holding someone accountable" as a strict way to enforce compliance, but as our team has walked together and been honest with each other, if anyone accuses one of us of, well, anything, the others can say, "Yes, we're aware of that, and we've been working with him on it." This form of accountability provides "vulnerable protection."

Years ago, I instituted a family form of accountability, but it was really just about me, not Amy or the kids. When our first son, Nathan, was born, I was terrified that I would treat him the way my father treated me. When he was just a young boy, I over-disciplined him. At one point, when he was still in diapers, I was spanking him too hard, and he called out, "Mom!" He was desperate for help. My heart broke because my little son realized he needed to be protected from me. Not long after that, I told Amy, and then as the children got older, I told each of them that they had complete permission to tell anyone absolutely anything I said or did. I wanted all of us to walk in the light. That's what stopped my dad from hurting me. It proved to be one of the best parenting moves I've ever made, but there were some odd moments.

When our third child, Sarah, was about six years old, we had recently moved to Colorado. When school started, she had a hard time getting up, getting dressed, and getting out the door. To motivate her, I played her favorite song, "Life Is a Highway," from the soundtrack of the Pixar movie *Cars*. I turned it up really loud and danced around in her room. She smiled and groaned, "Oh dad!" but I could tell she loved it. One morning as I was dancing to the music, I slapped my rear end, and said, "Come on, Sarah!" She got up and started dancing, slapping her rear end, too. She liked it so much that it became a regular part of our morning routine.

She knew the family rule that she could tell anybody anything at any time. One day I took Sarah along to a restaurant to meet with a musician I was recruiting for our worship team. He'd brought his wife, and I was trying to appear completely cool and confident. Sarah brought some coloring books and was working in them while the three adults talked. Suddenly, out of nowhere, she interrupted and asked, "Dad, why are you always whacking your butt in my face?" At that instant, I was mortified, but then I realized this was a beautiful moment — not for the couple, but for Sarah and me. Yes, I was embarrassed for a few minutes, but that was a small price to pay. When we got in the car, we laughed so hard. I told her, "Let's go home and tell your mom about it!" And we did. This saga in our family story went a long way to establish a culture of living in the light.

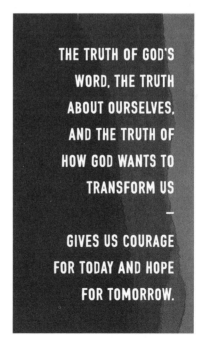

THE TRUTH OF GOD'S WORD, THE TRUTH ABOUT OURSELVES, AND THE TRUTH OF HOW GOD WANTS TO TRANSFORM US

—

GIVES US COURAGE FOR TODAY AND HOPE FOR TOMORROW.

SEXUAL SHAME

Perhaps the most punitive aspect of Christian culture is sexual shaming. God has made us complex beings with very strong desires and drives, including (and maybe especially) in the area of sex. In other areas of life—intellectually, physically, and relationally—we can grow and make mistakes without having them tarnish our reputations, at least not too badly, but we aren't as forgiving about any mistakes in our sexual lives. Sexual shame is a much more permanent stain. Adam and Eve used fig leaves to cover their shame. We use much more elaborate methods.

In an article for *Psychology Today*, sex therapist Diane Gleim observes, "Like fish swimming in the water, we are swimming in sexual shame, to the point where most of the time we are utterly oblivious to it. No one is immune from sexual shame, not even medical and mental health professionals. Sometimes a person's sexual shame is so ingrained and feels so much a part of their deepest self that they simply cannot imagine themselves without their shame."[21] She identifies several areas that often invoke feelings that are beyond embarrassment, including sexual body parts, powerful urges, uncontrolled daydreams, failed sexual attempts, and guilt over experiences of pleasure.

Don Schrader quipped, "To hear many religious people talk, one would think God created the torso, head, legs and arms, but the devil slapped on the genitals."[22] Studies show that the younger generation may feel more comfortable talking about sex, but surprisingly, they have less of it.[23]

I've told my sons, "If you want to be as dumb as your friends, talk only to them about important issues in your life. But if you want to be smart and get ahead of the game, talk to people a little older than you who have wisdom and experience. They're valuable resources for you." To illustrate my point, I use the history of the Ford-150. Over the years, I've seen hundreds, maybe thousands, of these trucks. From year to year, they have similar features, and when we look at the ones rolling off the assembly line today, we're looking at years of design history. And each year, the design history is clearly reflected in the new model. In the same way, people who have a long track record of insight see not only the current realities in culture, they also see the design history of how God has worked over time.

When my children were little, I wanted to "ruthlessly eliminate rebellion," but as I learned more about what makes people tick, my goal shifted to "ruthlessly eliminate shame." For that to happen, they would need to be able to ask any question about anything at any time . . . and for Amy and me to honor their curiosity instead of punishing them for asking about delicate topics.

Love and respect create a far healthier environment for growth than shame and the fear of punishment. That's true for families, teams, and every other relationship. God gave Adam and Eve only one rule along with a lot of attention and affirmation. Amy and I have tried to follow that example. We have very few rules, and we try to give our kids all the love, encouragement, meaningful conversations, fun, and time we possibly can. So far so good.

Instead of having "the sex talk" only once with Sam, our youngest, I told him that he can ask me anything about sex anytime he likes. We have an ongoing conversation about all kinds of things, and it appears he feels pretty comfortable with the arrangement because he asks all kinds of questions.

In every other area of life, we pursue best practices, we're open to new ideas, and we want to learn and grow, but in our sexual development, many of us hide like Adam and Even in the Garden. Curiosity is overwhelmed by insecurity and shame. Past failures may be steppingstones in other areas, but in our sexual lives, failures are millstones that crush us. The point I'm making is that even in marriages and close friendships, honesty about sex too often remains taboo . . . a secret. And secrets have a life of their own. Without the light of exposure and truth, they are the breeding ground for shame. I'm certainly not advocating that we publicly share elements of our sexual shame, but I'm certainly recommending that we don't take it off the table with the one we've chosen to trust with our secrets. No shame should remain hidden. Light needs to shine into the darkest places.

LETTING US IN

John records a long conversation Jesus had with His disciples on the night He was arrested. They had experienced His love for over three years, but at this moment, He wanted to make His relationship with them crystal clear. He told them something that stretches our ability to comprehend: "As the Father has loved me, so have I loved you."

Really? Jesus loves you and me in the same way the Father loves Him? It's astounding, and it would have been enough if He had stopped there. But He didn't stop. He told them they weren't a cistern to hold His love; they were rivers through which His love would flow: "My command is this: Love each other as I have loved you." How did Jesus love them? And by extension, how does He love us? He continued: "Greater love has no one than this: to lay down one's life for one's friends. You are my friends if you do what I command. I no longer call you servants, because a servant does not know his master's business. Instead, I have called you friends, for everything that I learned from my Father I have made known to you" (John 15:9, 12-15).

Jesus, Paul tells us in Colossians, is the creator of the universe. He lived in all eternity in immeasurable majesty, power, and glory, but He humbled himself to become one of us. He could have blasted the sinful world in divine judgment at any time, but instead, He bore the judgment we deserved. He could have made us cinders or slaves, but He calls us His friends.

Who were the "friends" He was talking to at that moment? Were they noble and righteous and good? Not exactly. Of the twelve, one betrayed Him, one denied Him, and one doubted Him. They ran and hid like scared little children when He was arrested. Only one, John, showed up at the cross.

Those who were closest to Him treated Him in ways that hurt Him, but He still called them "friends." True friendship doesn't mean we never hurt each other's feelings. It means we have a baseline commitment to be willing and able to listen and care . . . and to resolve hurt when it inevitably happens. Friendship isn't always comfortable. It requires courage and work. It even hurts sometimes because it's is a full-contact sport. But friendship is still totally worth it.

Jesus knew the hard realities about the people He called His "friends." Did the disciples plan to run away and leave Jesus to His fate? No, they saw

FRIENDSHIP ISN'T ALWAYS COMFORTABLE. IT REQUIRES COURAGE & WORK. IT EVEN HURTS SOMETIMES BECAUSE IT IS A FULL CONTACT SPORT. BUT FRIENDSHIP IS STILL TOTALLY WORTH IT.

themselves as faithful friends. Did Peter mean to deny Him? Of course not, yet his confident affirmation of loyalty, uttered only a few hours earlier, wilted when he was confronted by a servant girl. Jesus knew the worst about His disciples, and He loved them still. He knows the worst about you and me, too, and His love for us isn't diminished at all. He loves us like the Father loves Him. Amazing.

When we attempt to build strong relationships, we sometimes say things we don't intend to communicate. Years ago, our daughter Mady disobeyed Amy, and our discipline was to have her write twenty-five times, "I will obey my parents." Her younger sister Sarah suffers from a severe case of FOMO —fear of missing out — so she wanted to write the same sentence twenty-five times for fun. At the time, she was just learning to write, so Amy wrote the first line for her. A few minutes later, I checked on the girls' progress. Sarah had begun well. The first two lines were exactly right, but in the third line, one letter was wrong, and by the fifth, three letters were wrong. Her nineteenth to the end had morphed into the following statement: "I will obey my rats." Was she calling Amy and me rats? No, she communicated something she didn't really mean. How did it happen? She began with Amy as her reference point, but as she worked by herself, she lost the reference point and gradually slid into misstatements. She meant to write a respectful sentence, but the last few lines were unintentionally disrespectful.

The same thing happens to me sometimes, and my guess is that it happens to you, too. We intend to say something positive and true, but when we only have ourselves as a reference point, the words coming out of our mouths or through our email or social media posts unintentionally send the opposite message. We have to work hard to communicate what's really in our hearts—and sometimes, we need to first work hard on our hearts.

THE GIFT

Miss Molly earned her master's degree in counseling as a blind, single mother of a two-year-old. On the day of her graduation, one of her professors gave her a gift. She opened it and felt inside the box. It wasn't a familiar object. Her professor said, "Molly, it's a ratchet."

She laughed and responded, "What am I going to do with this?"

He explained, "In your counseling career, you'll find two kinds of people: Some people need a little tightening, and some people need a little loosening."

We don't know how to use the ratchet of compassion on someone until the proverbial nuts and bolts are brought into the light. Then we can clearly see what's too loose or too tight, and we can apply our love and truth in the most appropriate and constructive way.

I will obey my parents.
I will obey my parents.
I will obey my parents.
I will obey my proents.
I will obey my praents.
I will obey my praents.
I will obey my praents.
I will obey my raents.
I will obey my raets.
I will obey my raets.
I will obey my raets.
I will obey my raets.
I will obey my raets.
I will obey my raets.
I will obey my raets.
I will obey my raets.
I will obey my raets.
I will obey my raets.
I will obey my rats.
I will obey my rats.
I will obey my rats.
I will obey my rats.
I will obey my rats.
I will obey my rats.
I will obey my rats.

WITH MY GRANDMOTHER

WITH MY MOM, CAROLYN
2007

consider
THIS

1

What are some reasons living with "secrets in the dark" is attractive?

....

....

....

....

....

....

....

....

2

Why doesn't willpower alone work to enable us to overcome hidden patterns of sin and doubt?

....

....

....

....

....

....

....

....

3

In what ways is the light
of truth necessary for
spiritual, emotional,
and relational healing?

....

....

....

....

....

....

....

....

....

4

Do you think Christians
are more susceptible
than unbelievers
to sexual shame?
Explain your answer.

....

....

....

....

....

....

....

....

....

5

In what ways does Jesus'
commitment to be
friends with very flawed
people encourage you in
your relationships? Are
any changes needed?
If so, what are they?

....
....
....
....
....
....
....
....
....
....

6

Have you handed a
ratchet to anyone in
your life? If you have,
how is that person
using it to help you?
If you haven't, what's
your hesitation?

....
....
....
....
....
....
....
....
....
....

THE TRUTH IS
LIKE A LION:
YOU DON'T HAVE
TO DEFEND IT.
LET IT LOOSE:
IT WILL DEFEND
ITSELF.

— SAINT AUGUSTINE —

CHAPTER FIVE

GPS

When the annual Global Leadership Summit had a satellite location in Loveland, Colorado, a few years ago, I wanted to take my Brazilian friend and fellow Lion, Samuel Brum, so he could learn from some of the top leaders in the country. We were in a room with about 550 Northern Colorado pastors, staff, and business leaders. Each year, the coordinators invite experts to share their secrets of success, and this year they had asked Marcus Lemonis, entrepreneur and host of *The Profit*, a popular television program. He was known for his foul language, so the hosts told him he'd have to pay fifty dollars every time he swore, and he promised to give the money to a good cause. (It didn't seem to be much of an incentive.) During his talk, Lemonis said, "I wonder, are there any pastors in the audience who wish someone on your staff didn't work for you?" At that moment, faces flashed through my mind. I'd taken over a century-old church, and we had some staff members who had been on the ship long before I became the new captain. A couple of them were still working for us but were attending other churches. Actually, it wasn't hard to identify two or three who probably shouldn't still be on our team. Those thoughts happened in about a second. Then Lemonis said, "If that's you, stand up." I stood up. As I looked around, I had an excellent view of the 549 people who were still seated. Two thoughts instantly came to mind:

first, every other person in the room is a dirty, stinking liar, and second, I felt confident Lemonis would applaud my honesty and I'd be vindicated. That's not exactly what happened. The next words out of his mouth were, "Shame on you!"

Do you know the feeling in your throat right before you throw up? It was like someone had punched me in the gut and then gave me a karate chop in the esophagus. I could feel my ears flush, turn red, and get hot. In front of all of my peers, I looked like I belonged on another television show . . . *The Biggest Loser!* He never said "Sit down," maybe because he was sure no one had stood up. I wasn't going to stand a second longer, so I quickly sat down. I wanted to disintegrate, but that didn't happen either. Samuel felt my pain. He looked at me with a heart full of compassion and said in his Portuguese-laced English, "Bro, that was brutal."

As I was telling a friend about the message of this book, he asked, "Why do you think most people don't choose to be vulnerable?" This story is a snapshot of the answer: if we put ourselves out there, there's at least a fair chance we'll be deeply embarrassed.

THE STARTING POINT

Driving apps are a huge help to those of us who can easily lose our way, either trying to find a restaurant nearby or trying to get to the Pacific Ocean on a long trip. They work only when you include two points— your current location and your destination. If you don't put your current location, all you have is a map surrounding the destination without any directions to get there. This, I believe, is a good analogy of where many of us find ourselves in relationships. We can quote verses, we've read books, we've gone to conferences, and we've taught people how to have meaningful connections, but we haven't taken the time (or found the courage) to identify our current location. And quite often, we're stuck in the mud on some backroad while we're pretending to drive on the Interstate.

Some scholars think Machiavelli was the ultimate pessimist when he wrote *The Prince*, a description of the Medici rule in Florence in the sixteenth century, but I think he was a realist. His description of power grabs wasn't a view of the worst of human nature; it is human nature. He wrote, "How we live is so different from how we ought to live that he who studies what ought to be done rather than what is done will learn the way to his downfall rather than to his preservation." [24]

Here's my translation: We can only make progress if we're honest about where we are—in our most important relationships, our harbored resentments or forgiveness, our physical health, our mental health, and every other aspect of life. When we ask people, "How are you doing?" we almost invariably hear, "Fine," "Doing good," or something just as innocuous. I understand that the vast majority of people who ask how we're doing really don't want us to pour out our hearts at that moment, but we often give the same thoughtless answer when someone genuinely cares. Sometimes people give a response that's laced with guilt. I've asked guys, "How's your marriage?" and many of them quickly say things like: "You know, I really ought to be spending more time with my wife," or "I need to engage with her more on an emotional level," or "We should have more intimacy, but we're both so busy." They're focused on what should be instead of what is. They're not paying attention to their current location, so their emotional and relational GPS isn't the resource it could be.

WILD MOUNTAIN STALLION

I love images of wild horses that run free throughout parts of the West. They're beautiful, powerful, and unrestrained. From time to time, people are allowed to capture one of those horses, haul it back to their ranch, and begin breaking it. The process can be long and dangerous, but when it works, all the power and beauty of the wild horse is transformed into another version of power and beauty with someone in the saddle.

If, on the other hand, a colt is put in a tightly confined pen without room to run and grow strong, its growth will be stunted, its beauty lost, and its temperament dampened. When that horse is brought to a corral to be broken, the process only abuses the poor animal.

This comparison illustrates the impact of grace and law. Grace doesn't crush a person; it frees the person to be all God has created him or her to be. The experience of the love of God "breaks" us in the best possibly way, redirecting our energies and creativity to honor the One who loves us enough to die in our place and who credits His own righteousness to our account. If anything, we're more powerful, more dynamic, more passionate than ever before.

But the law doesn't have the same effect on us. It restricts, focuses on faults, and condemns. The law, Paul reminds us in Galatians, is a tutor that shows us our need for grace. The law is a cruel master, but it's a necessary starting point in our experience of grace.

In my conversations with Christians, I meet both kinds: wild mountain stallions who have been broken by the grace of God and now are beautiful and powerful with a transformed purpose, and those who act more like they've been in a cramped pen and beaten by their owners for many years. These perceptions shape everything we believe about God and ourselves, and they determine our willingness to be honest and vulnerable. A secure, confident stallion isn't threatened by hard truths, but those who are insecure can be devastated by even the mildest feedback, so they react disproportionately to it.

This analogy is another way to perceive where we are, our starting point in our journey to be whole, healthy, and connected. When we go back to the Garden, we see that the tree of life was strong on *what is* but light on what *should be*—in other words, strong on relationships and light on rules. In contrast, the tree of the knowledge of good and evil was strong on what *should be* and light on *what is*—heavy on rules and light on relationships. When Adam and Eve broke the one prohibition God had established, they tried to hide from Him and they covered up from each other in shame. Isn't that exactly what we do when we live only by the demands of the law? We no longer feel secure and confident enough to be honest. We try to hide from God, or we try to make up for our sin by pummeling ourselves with condemnation, and we're terrified of being vulnerable with others. We're living by law, not grace. Without grace, and without a relationship that communicates grace, we're left to figure things out on our own . . . and we're not very good at that!

THE LAW'S PURPOSE

It's odd that the most glorious gift ever given to mankind is so difficult to accept. Many of us don't really want grace; we want to prove ourselves. We want to earn God's approval . . . and for that matter, the approval of other people, too. The law brings us up to the window and lets us see into the glory of God, but it doesn't open the door. Only grace does that. We revere Moses, the one who brought the law of God down from the mountain, but he only brought the people close to the Promised Land, not into it.

During the first century, the Jewish religious leaders were certain that they were the righteous ones because they upheld the law during a difficult time of Roman occupation, when in fact, they added more rules to be sure people didn't get close to disobedience. But they completely missed Jesus, the embodiment of grace. They were so offended by Him and His message that they plotted to kill Him. To them, law was much more comfortable than grace. Their goal wasn't completely off-base. They wanted people to be holy and righteous, but their means was diametrically opposite from God's provision of grace.

The law acts as a guardrail that keeps us from falling off a cliff, but it's not the engine that gets us where God wants us to go. A loving, grace-filled relationship with God, and loving, grace-filled relationships with reliable people, are our sources of power, security, joy, and love. As we've seen, when Jesus was asked what is the greatest commandment in the law, His answer was that loving God and loving people is at the heart of God's purpose for us.

The law is the part of our GPS that shows us our starting point, but only if we pay attention. When we don't even look at it, all we see is a map around our destination. If we analyze many of the messages preached in churches every Sunday, we quickly realize most of them focus on what will be or what should be, not what is. We hear a lot about the ideal, but not as much about what's real. The solution isn't to stop talking about what will be and what should be—those are also important—but we need to do a better job of being ruthlessly honest about what is. When we look at Paul's magnificent letter to the Romans about the grace of God, we realize he spent most of the first three chapters describing our utter inability to make life work on our own. His description of what is, then, set the stage for the truth of grace and its application in the rest of the letter.

Let me tell the stories of two dads. They're brothers who grew up in an addictive home where their mom was strung out most of the time and their father was passive. Both of them suffered from their mother's violent outbursts when she was coming down off cocaine. One, I'll call him Richard, swore that he'd never treat his children the way either of his parents treated him. When his wife was pregnant with their first child, he thought long and hard and came up with some rigid rules for himself. He was determined to never scream at his children, to never hit them with his hands, and to use only a wooden spoon for spankings. The other brother, I'll call him Charles, had the same childhood experiences, but he made a very different commitment. Early and often, he would tell his children to be honest with him whenever they felt he was being overbearing. He still disciplined them, but each time, he reminded himself that his goal was to redirect them, not punish them.

Today, two of Richard's kids don't want to have anything to do with him. They believe he abused them, and they bear the emotional scars to prove it. Was he a better parent than his mother and father? Yes, certainly, but he didn't go far enough to replace harsh condemnation with loving correction. Charles's kids felt empowered when they were children, and as young adults, they know their father is their biggest fan.

That's a picture of the difference between law and grace. Law may have good intentions, but it can't melt and mold hearts with love. Grace calms, redirects, assures, and empowers. That's how Charles affected his children, and that's how God's grace affects you and me.

The law appeals to our old nature, our flesh, our desire to make life work apart from God. In Paul's piercing letter to the Galatians, he corrected them because they had drifted away from grace back into law as the basis of their relationship with God (and in determining who was acceptable for fellowship). Grace, he explained, gives us the freedom to love others, but the law creates competition, suspicion, and division: "You, my brothers and sisters, were called to be free. But do not use your freedom to indulge the flesh; rather, serve one another humbly in love. For the entire law is fulfilled in keeping this one command: 'Love your neighbor as yourself.' If you bite and devour each other, watch out or you will be destroyed by each other" (Galatians 5:13-15).

The flesh, though, doesn't surrender easily. It fights against grace! Paul told them to expect internal turmoil as they chose to live by God's grace: "So I say, walk by the Spirit, and you will not gratify the desires of the flesh. For the flesh desires what is contrary to the Spirit, and the Spirit what is contrary to the flesh. They are in conflict with each other, so that you are not to do whatever you want. But if you are led by the Spirit, you are not under the law" (vv. 16-18).

Paul's point—and by extension, my point—is that our desire to live by the law doesn't give up without a fight, and in fact, it doesn't give up until we see Jesus face to face. In the meantime, we're in a war between our natural bent toward comparison and the Spirit's pull toward love. One results in isolation; the other produces a heart of "love, joy, peace, forbearance, kindness, goodness, faithfulness, gentleness and self-control. Against such things there is no law" (vv. 22-23).

The journey begins (or picks up again) when we look at our GPS and figure out where we are in the battle between law and grace. Sometimes, just realizing we're in a fight lets us know that internal tension is normal. The "lions" on our team help one another figure out where we are so we can take steps in the right direction.

IDENTIFY WHAT IS

How can we determine our current location? Let me give a few suggestions.

★ FIND AND DEVELOP GREAT FRIENDSHIPS.

As we've seen, we tend to gravitate toward people who are much like us, with the same likes and dislikes, and the same blind spots. We're wise to establish some friendships with people who are very different from us, who see things from a different angle, and whose blind spots aren't on our radars. My best friends, Sethry and Zach, aren't like me, so they can help me navigate life and minimize the damage caused by my blind spots. A true friend is willing to speak into our lives when no one else will. These are "faithful wounds" that, like cuts from a surgeon's scalpel, result in healing. When we cultivate connections based on trust, we may hear some hard things, but we also experience sweetness. Solomon reflected, "Perfume and incense bring joy to the heart, and the pleasantness of a friend springs from their heartfelt advice" (Proverbs 27:9).

★ LEARN TO LIVE IN THE TENSION.

Most of us feel very uneasy until all our questions are answered and all our problems are solved. We see life as an equation we need to figure out instead of an adventure we take. When we jump too quickly to an answer, we often fail to fully appreciate the question. It may be more complex, and the answer may be richer, deeper, and more comprehensive. I would say that in marriage, parenting our kids, and all of our most important relationships, there's almost always a set of deeper questions underneath the one on the surface. If we answer the obvious one too quickly, we'll miss the others . . . and we'll miss the hearts of those people.

For example, while on a weekend retreat a few years ago, a man was sitting at a table with me and a group of my friends who are pastors. He listened as we griped about the problems of leading people and how often we feel misunderstood. After a long time, he asked, "Would you mind if I jump in?"

"No, please do," one of us responded.

"I have to tell you that as a church attender, I sometimes feel misunderstood by my pastor." He paused for a second to let his comment sink in, and then he said, "I read in Luke that a shepherd left the ninety-nine to go find the one and bring him back, but I wonder if my pastor would come find me if I was the one who wandered off." Again, he stopped for a few seconds. Then he asked, "I wonder, how far would each of you go to find the one and bring him back?"

One of the guys at the table immediately jumped in with something he'd read about the nature of sheep ("they're dumb") and how they need to be brought back against their will. As the pastor gave his answer, I thought, *He doesn't understand. This is a really profound question, and I'm pretty sure it would be wise to sit with it for a while.*

A couple of others offered on-the-spot answers, but I didn't feel comfortable saying anything. I thought about his question the rest of the day and into the night. The next morning at breakfast, I found him and said, "The question you asked kept me up last night. It's a great question, and not one that's easily answered . . . at least by me." I had come to the conclusion that quite often, simple answers are necessarily wrong because they don't do justice to the underlying complexities. I told him, "I have to admit that I don't know my answer to your question, but I'll probably spend the rest of my life trying to determine how far I'm willing to go to find the one who has wandered off and bring him back. It's a terrific question, and someday, I hope I'll have a terrific answer . . . In the meantime, I want to thank you for asking it."

He reached out and put his hand on my shoulder. He told me how he'd tried to be a friend to his pastor, but he couldn't get close. His pastor always had "the answer" to every question. He had felt belittled and marginalized. He told me, "Jonathan, the truth is that I wasn't looking for an answer when I asked him questions. I was looking for a touch." And he hugged me.

✴ WATCH YOUR WORDS.

I'm not talking about the four-letter variety; I'm talking about words that block or detour meaningful conversation. In the Christian subculture, we want to appear faithful and faith-filled, so we try really hard to be optimistic, especially when we're discouraged or anxious or angry. When we engage in "happy talk," how do others respond? Some, to be sure, are relieved that we aren't making them uncomfortable by being painfully honest; others see through our wall of smiling denial and determine that we aren't really trustworthy; and a few conclude that Christianity is a farce and look for something more authentic. Raising expectations that God will always come through in a way that makes us happy and comfortable leads to people crashing on the rocks of reality . . . and then, they have nowhere to turn. In his book, *Knowing God*, J. I. Packer warns that when we promise more than God intends to deliver, we're "cruel" to our listeners. [25]

I wonder what it would be like if we told people what's really going on. To be sure, some would feel uncomfortable with our honesty, but their comfort isn't our highest goal. Imagine how today's Christians might react to Jesus when He prayed in the Garden, "My soul is overwhelmed with sorrow to the point of death. Stay here and keep watch with me" (Matthew 26:38). I'm afraid a lot of people in our churches, including a lot of church leaders, would tell Him, "Just trust God. Remember Romans 8:28!"

Another example of raw honesty is found in the opening of Paul's second letter to the Corinthians. He wrote, "We do not want you to be uninformed, brothers and sisters, about the troubles we experienced in the province of Asia. We were under great pressure, far beyond our ability to endure, so that we despaired of life itself. Indeed, we felt we had received the sentence of death. But this happened that we might not rely on ourselves but on God, who raises the dead" (2 Corinthians 1:8-9). I can envision church people responding to him, "Oh Paul, it's not that bad! God has everything under control. Just trust Him."

I think our quick, simple answers are designed comfort ourselves more than the other person. We don't want to live in the tension. It's awkward, but genuine comfort requires us to enter the other person's emotional world and let our presence be the primary way we "answer" the other person's questions.

An organization asked me for advice to help pastors be more effective. I replied by explaining the problem of loneliness many pastors experience. I told them, "I'm sure there are some who need another idea about strategy, but most of them just need a friend. The words of a friend are patient, honest, and compassionate—not satisfied with superficial answers to life's most complex problems." As soon as I took a breath, a man in the room got up, made a face of obviously feigned compassion and walked over to give me a hug as he sarcastically said, "Oh Jonathan, I'm so sorry you're lonely." Everyone laughed, but they completely missed the point. Two years later, this organization started doing exactly what I recommended, and with great effect. Today, it's a hallmark of their values, strategy and culture. Still, the way the man responded to me is the kind of superficial response that minimizes the person and the issue.

★ REALIZE THAT SOME PEOPLE SIMPLY AREN'T SAFE TO CONFIDE IN.

No, they're not going to pull out a machete and attack you, but they aren't capable of entering your world and sitting with you long enough to truly understand what's going on in your life. Jesus escaped from people who were eager to harm Him (John 10:31-39), and Paul warned Timothy to avoid Alexander the coppersmith (2 Timothy 4:14). If you have a track record of trusting untrustworthy people, find a professional who can help you make better choices.

★ LET PEOPLE ASK HARD QUESTIONS ABOUT MATTERS OF FAITH.

We do people a great disservice by communicating that all the basic questions of faith have been sufficiently answered and put to bed . . . and it rings alarm bells when people, especially pastors, still have these questions. In recent years, a number of high-profile church leaders have abandoned the faith. Some have become agnostic, and a few are now antagonistic toward Christianity. I wonder if they had questions but didn't feel safe voicing them...until it was too late. We need to create a safe place where people feel free to ask their nagging questions — especially the ones they've been afraid to ask because they might be labeled heretics!

Some pop culture icons — including Seth Meyers, Ricky Gervais, and Bill Maher, among others — regularly challenge the presuppositions of Christian faith. They question the doctrines of creation, the reality of heaven and hell, the authority of the Bible, the integrity of the Christian right in politics, and countless other topics. Quite often, their questions are valid and deserve a carefully reasoned response, but it's difficult to offer one when we live in a Christian culture that makes even asking those questions seem wrong. The problem is more with us than with them.

Quite often, professors of theology seem dogmatic and rigid, while their students thoughtfully probe for truth. Bright students are having problems finding satisfying answers because some of their teachers lack intellectual curiosity. The illusion created in the minds of some students is that the Bible doesn't stand up to scrutiny, when in reality, it's the professor's limited view that doesn't. We've made apologetics the bedrock of our faith, but we need to remember that the disciples followed Jesus even though they were clueless about His theology most of the time. Their relationship with Him is what kept them going, not having all the answers. (And by the way, the Pharisees thought they had all the answers, and look where that got them!)

When people ask me questions about the authority of the Bible, creation and evolution, and a host of other topics, I make a point of not giving "the answer" too quickly. If I attempt to be "the guy who has all the answers," the conversation becomes more about me than about the other person, or even God. Instead, I often say, "That's a great question, and people have come up with several ways to look at it." And I help them explore the possibilities and develop or clarify their own viewpoints.

For instance, some have asked, "Jonathan, how do you know God exists?" I could go through Aquinas's five "proofs" that God exists or explain Pascal's wager that it makes more sense to believe in God than not. But instead, I respond, "I don't. I'm not a 'knower,' I'm a 'believer.'" At its bedrock, my faith rests on a relationship with God made real through Jesus. I give people the same permission to believe when they don't absolutely know all the answers, and for some, that's all they need to start a walk of faith.

When someone asks me a hard question about faith, I want to first affirm their willingness to ask, and then I often ask my own questions to find out why they're asking. My goal isn't to whip them back in line, so my strategy isn't corrective.

Invite people to ask any question they want to ask, and try not to respond in horror or offer simplistic answers, and they'll probably find enough reason to remain strong in their faith over the long haul. But if we don't provide a safe and welcoming environment, their questions will go unasked and unanswered, and they'll look to Bill Maher as a safer, smarter resource than church leaders.

Over the years, I've found that many believers feel deeply discouraged that they aren't making more progress in their spiritual journeys. They're not the husbands, wives, sons, daughters, fathers, and mothers they know they should be. Far too often, their solution is to deny what's happening or bludgeon themselves for being so bad—or if they're gifted and creative, they do both! I want to help them discern where they are, to identify not just the surface status, but also the underlying condition. When they have a starting point for their GPS, they can then make real progress.

consider
THIS

1

Are you so positive and optimistic that you're not objective about what's real? How can you know if that's true for you?

....

....

....

....

....

....

....

2

Who helps you identify your blind spots? Are you open to their feedback? Would your best friend say you're open?

....

....

....

....

....

....

....

....

3

What are some ways
the demands of the
law help us identify
our current position?

....

....

....

....

....

....

....

....

....

4

What are some
consequences of
trying to obey the
law without turning
to grace as a source
of transformation?

....

....

....

....

....

....

....

....

....

5

Who do you know who "lives in the tension" of unanswered questions and unsolved problems? Are you learning anything from that person? Explain your answer.

....
....
....
....
....
....
....
....
....

6

How comfortable are you with letting people wrestle with matters of faith?

....
....
....
....
....
....
....
....
....
....

To Jonathan +
Hunting +
Hanging Together!
Your friend
[signature]

PHEASANT HUNTING
WITH JOHN MAXWELL

SEPTEMBER 2020

IF WE ARE

GROWING

WE ARE ALWAYS

GOING TO BE

OUTSIDE OUR

COMFORT

ZONE.

— JOHN C. MAXWELL

CONGRATULATIONS
CLASS OF

MADELYN'S GRADUATION
May 2018

FUJI RDP III   14

20A

HUNTING WITH FRIENDS
SEPT 2019

CHAPTER SIX

FIRST STEPS

In the Introduction, I said a little bit about a life-changing retreat I experienced, and how I've ever since been applying what I learned there. In this chapter, I want to go into a bit more detail.

The retreat center in Montana is in a beautiful setting in the mountains, beside a lake with rivers nearby. The schedule was wide open. If people wanted to fish, they had their choice of spots; if they wanted to see a movie, they could drive into town and do that; and if they wanted to just walk about and enjoy the scenery, that was fine, too. The only requirement was to attend a family dinner each night. About twenty of us sat around a large table with heaping plates of delicious food prepared by an amazing chef and served by an incredible team. Some of the guys came with a friend, but most of us were flying solo and were meeting each other for the first time.

On the first night, we were asked to share our answers to a single question: "What's your high point and your low point right now?" (One pastor paraphrased it: "What's making you happy and what makes you feel crappy?") The men could choose the depth of vulnerability. The first two or three kept it safe. They said something like, "Oh man, our church is growing. We're seeing God do amazing things. My wife and I love each other more than ever. Life's good." But eventually one man took a risk to reveal what was really going on . . . and the next guy followed his lead . . . and the next and the next. Men talked about their depression, the strain their ministries were taking on their marriages, problems with kids, an alarming diagnosis, or conflict on a team or with a board. It only took one courageous individual to open the door. After that, the rest of the guys had a green light to share their fears and hopes . . . and the first couple of guys wanted a do-over. They didn't want to miss out on the support the rest of the men were experiencing from each other.

During the days, conversations that were begun the night before continued as we found people who identified with us and had compassion for us. By the fourth and last night, we became close friends, and the friendships have lasted ever since. We had bared our souls, and nobody laughed, nobody condemned, and nobody ran away. We felt safe, known, and profoundly cared for. It was incredible.

As the days progressed, I noticed a pattern in our group that I suspect was true of every group that spent four days together at the retreat center. The leaders had hit on a process that was inviting, but not demanding. They let guys go deeper as they chose, and the environment created strong bonds of friendship. By the time we left, I wanted to support the retreat center, and I wanted to find a way to replicate the impact in the lives of every church leader I know. But how?

On the last night, Greg Surratt, a pastor from Mt. Pleasant, South Carolina, was sitting with his best friend. Greg said something that shook up the presuppositions of a lot of the pastors in the room: "Don't think you have to be isolated in your church. People say, 'It's lonely at the top,' but it doesn't have to be." He nodded toward his friend and continued, "My best friend goes to my church. I know that goes against conventional wisdom, but sometimes conventional wisdom needs to be challenged."

His comment ignited some new ideas, or more accurately, posed some fresh questions. One of the reasons the retreat center experience worked was that most of us didn't know each other, so we felt safe being open. But what if this could work on a staff team . . . with small groups . . . in marriages . . . with friends back home? Actually, I didn't know I needed this level of honest connections until I experienced it. I wondered, *Do the people on our staff team even know they need it? Can we replicate what happened at the retreat center in our relationships? Do we even want to?*

CAN IT WORK HERE?

When I got back home, I told three of our veteran staff members about my experience. They could tell I was really excited about what had happened. Then I asked, "Do you think we could create something like this on our team?"

All of them shook their heads. One spoke for the group, "Uh, no, Jonathan. I don't think so."

When I asked "Why?" he explained, "Well, it's because we work for you. I can't imagine telling you things that might show up in a performance review."

Another one chimed in, "And besides that, I sure don't want others on our team to know my secrets!"

And the third told me, "And I don't want the people I lead to know every-thing about me. I'm afraid gossip would ruin my relationships with them."

There was pushback on three levels: "I don't want you to know too much about me," "I don't want *my peers* to know," and "I don't want *the people I lead* to know." Points taken.

At that moment, I realized I needed to make some adjustments to adapt what I'd experienced at the retreat center to our team. I thanked them for their input, and I went to my office to write a detailed process of how our team could at least approach more meaningful connections. I began writing, and I identified the steps in the next five chapters of this book: Relate, Trust, Disclose, Process, and Integrate. I sent it to twelve of our staff members and asked them to consider taking steps forward with me one-on-one, not in a group, with nothing forced, no condemnation for reluctance, and the promise of confidentiality. I explained that I would take the initiative for the first conversation, but after that, the initiative and pace would be entirely up to them. Our talks, I told them, wouldn't be about ministry per-formance and progress—that's a different conversation. Instead, these talks would be about their fears and hopes, their struggles and triumphs. All of them agreed. Their "yes" proved to be a catalyst for health and growth in our organization.

My commitments are to the men on our staff; my wife Amy has similar con-nections with the women. It's not wise to have men with women in these self-disclosing conversations. Amy leads the leaders who are women. I lead the men. Both groups are thriving.

When we started, the guys on our team were understandably reluctant to go below the surface. I didn't push at all, but soon they began peeling off layers of defensiveness to be more open. They wanted to tell me about current struggles and past hurts. When I listened carefully and asked follow-up questions, they gradually were convinced I was a safe person, so they peeled off another layer.

My primary goal in these conversations isn't to conform the people on the team to my standards or make them more productive in ministry, although we've found that one of the results of this process is greater effectiveness in leading people. Instead, my intention is to help them achieve their goals, especially in their most important relationships. I want to help them thrive in their relationship with God and with their families, and to thrive, people often need to address hindrances they've ignored (or been intimidated by) for a long, long time. In this role, I see myself more as an older brother who wants to help his siblings genuinely experience and authentically express God's love.

In our culture, most of our relationships are transactional: I'll do this for you if you'll do that for me. But in these conversations, no one owes me anything. Paul told the Romans, "Owe nothing to anyone except to love one another; for he who loves his neighbor has fulfilled the law" (Romans 13:8 NASB). The guys on my team don't owe me their secrets. They're not obligated in the least to disclose anything they don't want to tell me. They have the same permission I give my kids: they can tell me anything at any time, so if there's even a hint of my pushing where they don't want to go, I want them to tell me. And at that moment, my commitment is to thank them for their honesty, not to sneer at them for not being open with me. I meet with them weekly to talk about their roles at the church, but our one-on-ones about their hearts are entirely at their invitation. If I don't hear from them about the next conversation, that's fine with me. As I spent time helping one of our guys deal with a very sticky family issue, at one point he told me, "Jonathan, I don't think I can take this right now. I need a break. I'll let you know when I'm ready to dive in again."

I responded, "Great. I'll be ready when you are."

I don't see myself as the savior to fix the emotional and relational distress of the guys on our team. I'm just one resource for them. The Holy Spirit usually prompts a number of people to provide care, encouragement, and support for those who are struggling. Similar to what I experienced at the retreat center, God leads us to others who may have had similar wounds, and we find understanding where we didn't expect it. It's a beautiful thing to see.

It would probably be helpful to hear from a couple of the guys on our team of lions.

Sethry Connor is an associate lead pastor at Rez.

When Jonathan came back from the retreat and asked how we could use the process on our team, I was one of those who said, "No way! You guys had the benefit of anonymity. You aren't going to see each other again, except maybe across the room at a conference. We see each other every day!"

But I could tell something was on fire in Jonathan, so I told him, "I'll be glad to try to work this out with you, but it'll take at least five years to break the surface."

I didn't understand that he was offering one-on-one talks, not sharing in a group, and I didn't understand that we would have total control over when we shared with him, what we shared, and how quickly we went to the next level of openness. It didn't take five years. Within about six months, the vibe on our team was incredibly positive. God was doing some really good things in a lot of lives: healing hurts, assuring people of forgiveness, and relieving a lot of tension in other relationships.

The benefits go far beyond my relationship with Jonathan and the others on our team. My son is going into middle school, with all the craziness that involves, and we've had some wonderful conversations. I realized I didn't have to cram everything I wanted to say into a single conversation. The first one was just the beginning, and we've had many more terrific talks about all kinds of things he faces at school and with his friends.

My background in church is long and strict, some would call it Puritanical, others might use the word Pharisaic. I didn't want my son to be stunted by my deeply ingrained presumptions, so I took him on a trip so we could talk without distractions. In one of our conversations, I told him, "There are going to be things that happen that are really hard. I want you to know that if you ever need to tell me anything or ask anything, I won't punish you for being honest. I want to walk with you through this season of your life. There's nothing you can say or do that will disappoint me or diminish my love for you." As he grows through his middle school and high school years, as he becomes a young adult, finds a purpose and a career, and when he gets married and has children, I hope my love and my example will shape every relationship in his life. I sincerely doubt I would ever have had that kind of relationship with my son if Jonathan hadn't created that kind of connection with me.

My wife Christine and I have been able to talk about things we'd avoided for years. On one level, our honesty has surfaced some pain in our marriage, but it had been there all along. We had just been avoiding it. But surfacing those things has resulted in understanding, healing, and more love than ever. Our marriage wasn't bad before, but now we're more honest with each other, so we don't hide and pose nearly as much. Our love for each other is genuinely for each other, not for just an image we've tried to project. This process is disruptive, but in a very good way. It offers opportunities for relationships to grow stronger and deeper.

The people on our team are really supportive of each other. When someone has a problem, he doesn't have to hide it. He can be open and honest, and the rest of us help carry the load. It's comforting to know no one is alone, no one has to hide, and no one will be criticized for having a problem. We used to compete with each other to compensate for our insecurities, but now we celebrate every win. It's amazing how great it feels to walk through our offices and in our services because we know we're loved and accepted.

Far too often, the church is a shame culture with rigid expectations and harsh condemnation. What if we had more of the kind of relationships Jonathan has created on our team and I've built with my family?

Jonathan has modeled the blend of safety and vulnerability—that's a powerful combination—and he has made himself available when anyone feels the need to talk. He often writes his sermons at five o'clock in the morning because he's been talking to one of us when he would normally prepare, but his messages haven't suffered from his shifting schedule. In fact, he's more insightful, more compassionate, and has even better applications . . . but he never uses any of us as juicy illustrations!

Jonathan invited a group of us who are on staff to hang out at a cabin in the mountains for a few days. I'd never been on a retreat without an agenda to accomplish specific goals, but Jonathan's "specific goal" was for us to just get to know each other. It was the most profound spiritual experience of my life. We prayed together with more honesty and compassion than I'd ever experienced. We wept together, and we laughed together. And it wasn't just Jonathan speaking into people's lives. In that environment, we experienced true "one another" connections, and we felt loved and encouraged by everyone there. We experienced what I'd call "synergistic strength." These are the people I get to work with every day! At one point, it felt like heaven was touching earth. It didn't happen because we had an A-list speaker and were wowed by a message. It happened when guys were willing to be real with each other, and the Spirit of God met us there.

Zach Crider is an associate lead pastor and worship arts ministry leader at Rez.Church.

Before Jonathan told us about his time at the Montana retreat, I didn't let anyone know what was going on with me. But when he told us about his ideas, I was excited about them. I wanted a life coach, someone who wasn't focused only on my performance as a worship leader but would see me as a person on a journey. To be honest, it was a little scary to think that my boss was the one who was willing to walk with me.

Early in our conversations, I asked Jonathan, "How do we know which step we're on in the process? What's the right pace?"

He said, "You tell me. It's entirely up to you. We can move as fast or as slow as you feel comfortable."

I remember Jonathan telling me, "Guilt can be healthy, but shame never is. Guilt is the feeling of doing something wrong; shame is believing we are something wrong." It was very helpful to separate those. I realized a lot of my hiding came from feelings of shame.

I love my work, but I saw that my desire to do a great job at the church was taking away from my relationships with my wife and my two little boys. I told some of the guys on our team about this struggle, and they've been really supportive. And things at home have changed a lot. Before, when I came home, my kids would say "Hey, Dad" and go back to what they'd been doing, but now they run over to hug me and we play for an hour or so. That may seem like a small change, but it's huge to me . . . and I suspect, for my sons.

For a long time, I was more concerned with the production of the people on the worship team than caring about them as people, but that has changed, too. I've adopted the leadership philosophy of Kim Scott, an author and CEO coach: "Care personally, challenge directly, with radical candor." [26] This says, "I'm on your side. I'm your ally. What are your wins on our team? What are your wins at home? How can I help?"

I've had some big questions about my faith, and when I shared them with Jonathan, he wasn't alarmed at all. I'd had them for a long time, but I was afraid to tell anyone. He helped me work through them, accept the tension that I couldn't be certain about everything, and relax with those uncertainties.

I'm healthier spiritually, my work life is heathier, and my family relationships are healthier. What's not to like about that?

MAYBE YOU, MAYBE NOT

I feel like I need to include a warning label at this point: "The process outlined in this book can be threatening. Proceed with caution!" Let me be honest. I've known plenty of pastors and other church leaders who definitely shouldn't use the principles in this book because they have a track record of being much more of a CEO than a shepherd. I've also known some tenderhearted pastors who have stepped into a church where the staff and board members have felt burned and are very defensive. So, you may not be the right person to lead this process, or your situation may not be conducive to your leading it . . . at least not yet.

Even in the best of circumstances, proceed slowly. Introduce the concepts, assure people that you won't push at all, and explain that they have control over the depth and the speed of openness. Don't be surprised when some people are too eager to be self-disclosing while others remain resistant for a long time. You probably have the full spectrum of responses on your team or in your group.

If you haven't worked through a measure of your own pain, fears, grief, and doubts, you won't be able to comfort others with the comfort God has given you. Your first step, then, is to find a coach or mentor who will patiently give you an open door to surface your fears and dreams and help you overcome your inclination to deny, minimize, and excuse.

If you feel like you need to have all the answers or you need to be the hero to your team, stop and take stock of your motives. Your role isn't to solve every problem so the people on your team will develop a dependence on you. Your role is to help them grow stronger so they can pass these practices to many others.

If your goal for this process is to make your team more efficient, stop. You've missed the whole point. This isn't about production; it's about creating an environment where we call each other *friend* . . . and mean it. Lions work together to bring down prey so they can feast . . . they don't eat each other.

And always remember: Throughout this process, the gas pedal and the brake aren't where the leader sits. They're on the passenger's side.

consider
THIS

1

After reading the first half of the book, and especially this chapter, what are your hopes and fears about introducing this process in your most important relationships?

....

....

....

....

....

....

....

2

Why is it important that "no one owes anything but to love one another"?

....

....

....

....

....

....

....

3

What are the limits of
your relational expertise,
interest in helping
others, and capacity
to get involved in their
lives? (All of us have
limits. That's not a flaw
. . . just a reality.)

···
···
···
···
···
···
···
···
···

4

Did the stories from
Sethry and Zach
answer any questions
for you? If so, what
were they? Do you still
have some questions?
Who can help you
find the answers?

···
···
···
···
···
···
···
···
···
···

5

The last section of the chapter has a warning label and several "ifs." Which of these, if any, apply to you? Explain your answer.

....

....

....

....

....

....

....

....

....

....

....

....

....

....

....

....

....

....

....

....

FIVE STAGES OF CONNECTION

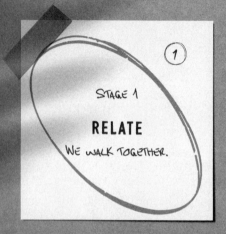

STAGE 1

RELATE

WE WALK TOGETHER.

STAGE 2

TRUST

WE SHARE OUR STORIES.

STAGE 3

DISCLOSE

WE CONFESS OUR FAULTS
TO EACH OTHER.

STAGE 4

PROCESS

WE SUBMIT TO EACH OTHER.

STAGE 5

INTEGRATE

WE ACCEPT GOD'S GRACE.

CHAPTER SEVEN

RELATE

This is the point in the book where we turn the corner and begin exploring the five stages of open, honest communication. Let me give a quick overview:

☀ STAGE 1 ⟶ RELATE ☀

WE WALK TOGETHER.

☀ STAGE 2 ⟶ TRUST ☀

WE SHARE OUR STORIES.

☀ STAGE 3 ⟶ DISCLOSE ☀

WE CONFESS OUR FAULTS TO EACH OTHER.

☀ STAGE 4 ⟶ PROCESS ☀

WE SUBMIT TO EACH OTHER.

☀ STAGE 5 ⟶ INTEGRATE ☀

WE ACCEPT GOD'S GRACE.

We begin by relating and getting to know each other.

> MANY TIMES, THE GUYS ON
> OUR TEAM AND I WALK
> TOGETHER BY LITERALLY
> WALKING TOGETHER...
> PHYSICALLY WALKING
> WITH SOMEONE REQUIRES
> ATTENTION TO PACE AND
> RHYTHM SO TWO CAN
> WALK SIDE BY SIDE.

Aristotle was a pretty smart guy. He had insights about all kinds of things, including relationships. He identified three kinds of friendships based on their purposes. He says we have "friendships of utility" because people are useful to us. This is the barista at the coffee shop who knows what we're going to order when we walk through the door. We have "friendships of pleasure" with people who share similar interests. This is the guy who cheers for our favorite team and discusses the game with us the next day. And we have "perfect friendships." These are the relationships that make life worth living. Love is shared without manipulation or unrealistic expectations, with no strings attached.[27] We have a lot of friendships of utility, some friendships of pleasure (especially if we're extroverts), but only a few perfect friendships. Those are treasures, and like we learn from any good adventure story, treasures can be hard to find.

The first step into meaningful, rewarding relationships is simply to relate. This is friendship on the lowest shelf. We're not expecting people to be vulnerable. We're just hanging out. We might think of this stage as the beginning of a friendship of pleasure because we're starting to learn what we have in common.

For Sethry and me, it started with Topgolf on Tuesdays. Topgolf is half-price on Tuesdays, and Sethry loves to find deals. We found a cheap and fun way to get to know each other. The time can be scheduled or spontaneous, as long as it's reasonably frequent. I shoot for once a week. Of course, I can't do this with twenty men, so even this step is selective.

Many times, the guys on our team and I walk together by literally walking together. Some of them must have been speed walkers in the Olympics because they get ahead of me in an instant. Even Amy sometimes gets going so fast that I call to her, "Hey, if you want to walk that fast, you'll be walking alone!" . . . which is a fun way to say, "Honey, please slow down and wait for me." The point is that *physically* walking with someone requires attention to pace and rhythm so two can walk side by side. In the same way, people who want to walk together relationally need to find a comfortable pace — not too fast or too slow. They also need a good rhythm, usually a weekly connection for friends and more than that for family. Quite often, both people have to make some adjustments so they can walk comfortably together.

Proximity and pleasant conversation are the goals of this stage, if you can call them goals. Just being together and talking about interesting things is plenty at this point in the process . . . no pressure at all.

Let me give a warning about "interesting things." In our fiercely polarized political culture, we walk through fields with sticks of dynamite at every step. The fuses are sticking out, and all it takes is one spark to set off a series of explosions. I've seen normally calm, thoughtful people, react in rage when someone mentions a politician's name, how different parties view the pandemic, Black Lives Matter, gun ownership, abortion, immigration, and other hot topics. I'm not saying you should avoid these issues, but I'm certainly saying that you need to be sure you're not on fire if you choose to walk among the sticks of dynamite! Inciting fury isn't the way to have easygoing connections with people.

Who is walking with you?

THE PROPHETS' CHOICE

The historian who wrote the two books of Kings in the Old Testament described Elijah as a mighty prophet. One of the most dramatic scenes in the Bible is "the battle of the gods" on Mount Carmel between him and the prophets of Baal. First, the prophets built an altar and went through an elaborate and bloody ritual as they called Baal to answer them, but there was only silence. Elijah taunted them, asking if Baal was asleep or in the bathroom. When they finally gave up, Elijah built a large altar of stone and wood, put pieces of a bull on it, and drenched it all three times. (I can almost hear Elijah tell them, "Now it's my turn. Stand back and watch this!") When he called on the Lord, fire came down from heaven and consumed the bull, the wood, the stones, the dirt around the altar, and even all the water was instantly evaporated! The triumph was complete with the deaths of Baal's prophets.

It was, no doubt, an incredible moment of God honoring a person's faith, but Elijah's euphoria didn't last long. King Ahab and Queen Jezebel sent a message threatening his life. He had boldly faced the threat of hundreds of prophets, but a letter from Jezebel caused him to run away. While on the run, he asked God to take his life, but after a long sleep, an angel woke him and gave him a good meal. He was reinvigorated, and he walked forty days to Mount Horeb.

Still, Elijah's discouragement hadn't lifted. He felt sorry for himself. To convince Elijah of His presence, God sent a wind like a hurricane, an earthquake, and a fire, but Elijah was still discouraged. He told God, "I have been very zealous for the LORD God Almighty. The Israelites have rejected your covenant, torn down your altars, and put your prophets to death with the sword. I am the only one left, and now they are trying to kill me too"

(1 Kings 19:14). God assured Elijah that he wasn't alone, and in fact, there were seven thousand faithful people who still were loyal to Him.

Elijah left Mount Horeb and found Elisha, who was supervising the plowing of his field with twelve yoke of oxen. As a sign of validation, Elijah threw his cloak around the young man. Wait a minute: Elisha didn't ask for the cloak, and I can imagine being draped with a heavy cloak on a hot day was the last thing he wanted, but he realized he had been selected for something special. Elisha knew at this moment that "the old had passed away; behold, the new has come," so he prepared the twenty-four oxen for a barbecue for the people in his community, and he left to be Elijah's servant. (See 1 Kings 19.)

The two men walked together until it was time for Elijah to depart . . . and he wasn't going to leave in any conventional way, like death or exile. Elisha knew this was the day his mentor would be leaving him. Elijah told him to stay while he walked to Jericho, but the younger man insisted, "As surely as the Lord lives and as you live, I will not leave you" (2 Kings 2:4).

Fifty other prophets stood at a distance, watching the scene unfold. Elijah struck the waters of the Jordan with his cloak, and it divided to allow him and Elisha to cross on dry ground. Elijah asked Elisha if he had one last request, and the young prophet told him, "Let me inherit a double portion of your spirit" (v. 9). Then Elisha witnessed a phenomenal sight:

> As they were walking along and talking together, suddenly a chariot of fire and horses of fire appeared and separated the two of them, and Elijah went up to heaven in a whirlwind. Elisha saw this and cried out, "My father! My father! The chariots and horsemen of Israel!" And Elisha saw him no more. Then he took hold of his garment and tore it in two. (2 Kings 2:11-12)

We can draw several applications from looking at this story:

 FIRST, PAY ATTENTION TO THE DIVINE FLOW.

I'm sure you've tried to connect with some people, only to have the conversation fall flat. I think everyone has. But most of us have also met someone (maybe several someones) and realized, "Man, this person really gets me!" I think of those people like the words I highlight with a yellow marker in a book or my Bible. It's as if God is highlighting that person, indicating that this connection is in the divine flow. Your destiny can be unlocked by investing in special relationships like this.

Elijah's cloak was infused with the anointing of the Holy Spirit, and when it touched Elisha's shoulders, he knew something very special was happening. That's how I've felt when I've been touched by a few of the people God has brought into my life.

SECOND, EVEN IN THE DIVINE FLOW, THE CONNECTION MAY RUN INTO DIFFICULTIES.

I didn't mention this earlier, but Elisha's first reaction to the life-changing moment of receiving the cloak wasn't, "I'm yours. I'll go anywhere you want to go, and I'll do anything you tell me to do." Instead, he planned an instant detour: "Let me kiss my father and mother goodbye, and then I will come with you." Elijah had been disappointed before, and it appears he was disappointed again. I can almost see the frown on his face when he told the young man, "Go back. What have I done to you?" (1 Kings 19:20)

That's the moment Elisha cut all ties with his past by cooking oxen steaks over the fire built from his plows and other equipment. When the dinner was over, he followed Elijah.

When we think we've found a new friend, we may hit some bumps in the road . . . and we may hit them as we're pulling out of the parking lot. Don't be surprised when other priorities, schedules, and previous commitments seem to prevent the friendship from moving forward. But also, don't give up. Give it time, and see if God keeps things moving.

(3) THIRD. PRIORITIZE GODLY RELATIONSHIPS.

Elijah had been the consummate Lone Ranger. He had only one servant as he faced down the 450 prophets of Baal, he was alone as he ran from Queen Jezebel, he was alone when God sent the wind, the earthquake, and the fire, and he was alone on his forty-day trek to Mount Horeb. When people are alone for a long time, they develop assumptions and habits that reinforce their isolation. When Elijah and Elisha met in the young man's field, both of them had to make major adjustments. The question for them and for us is simple: What's the cost-benefit ratio of the new connection? In other words, is it worth it to change priorities and schedules?

(4) FOURTH. DON'T CREATE "ICKY DEPENDENCE."

You can borrow my term any time you want to. I'm sure you know what I'm talking about. This kind of unnatural need and unhealthy control comes from either direction, or both. Some people come from very difficult backgrounds and are too quick to latch on to someone, and they latch on too tightly. They lose themselves in the life of someone else—perhaps a powerful leader or a pitiful person who plays the role of a victim. I've also known leaders who insist on making every decision, who dominate their teams and their families, and whose idea of leadership is all about their own power and position.

Elijah didn't create that kind of connection with Elisha. You certainly can't say their relationship was overly dependent. Scholars estimate they worked together for six to eight years. At the beginning, even after Elisha affirmed, "I'm all in," Elijah gave him the freedom to walk away. And at the end, Elijah attempted to distance himself from his protégé. Was that harsh? Unfeeling? Self-focused? My guess is that the older prophet didn't want to make things too easy for Elisha. He was well aware of the hardships of leadership, and he was testing Elisha one more time. Then again, it's possible that Elijah was grieving because he knew it was his last day with Elisha, and like many of us, when we're really sad, we push people away.

I prefer for God to put people in my life to constantly affirm me and tell me how great I am (or at least that I'm not too much of a mess), but some of the most important relationships in my life are with people who aren't shy about challenging me. These aren't connections of icky dependence; they're robust and life-changing.

Elisha's commitment to Elijah wasn't based on convenience. When he left home by making the dramatic statement of burning equipment and having the oxen for dinner, he dedicated himself first to God and then to Elijah. That's the right pattern. In fact, when we see the old prophet try to push Elisha away at the end, Elisha tells him emphatically, "As surely as the Lord lives and as you live, I will not leave you." That's a commitment oriented first in God and then in each other.

Walking with someone isn't always pleasant, but it can be anointed by God to accomplish more than we can imagine.

(5) ## FIFTH, LISTEN TO THE RIGHT KIND OF ADVICE.

The story tells us there were two groups of prophets who were watching Elijah and Elisha from a distance on the older man's last day on earth. One group came from Bethel. They knew that Elijah would be taken that day, and they asked Elisha, "Do you know that the Lord is going to take your master from you today?" (2 Kings 2:3) The implication is, "He's leaving, and you're obviously the new anointed guy, so there's no need to follow him any longer."

I love Elisha's response to their misplaced advice: "Yes, I know, so be quiet" (v. 3). They were right in their prophetic understanding that it was Elijah's last day, but they were wrong about the connection between the two men. The Bethel prophets didn't understand the bond between Elijah and Elisha. I've seen similar misunderstandings too many times in the church: We can be so focused on accomplishing goals for God that we forget every goal is about people, and the means of accomplishing every goal is the body of Christ working in harmony to honor Him.

Do we need a vertical relationship with God? Of course, but even a casual reading of the Bible emphasizes the necessity of meaningful horizontal connections. Jesus, the perfect God-man, almost constantly spent time with people. In fact, the only time we see Him withdrawing was to spend time with the Father, and then He connected with people again. He didn't hide from people even when they annoyed Him or hurt His feelings— though there were plenty of times when they tried to do that!

(6) SIXTH. SOME PEOPLE PREFER TO STAY ON THE SIDELINES.

A second group of prophets, fifty of them, "stood at a distance, facing the place where Elisha had stopped at the Jordan" (v. 7). They watched as Elijah struck the water with his cloak and the two men walked to the other side, but these prophets didn't walk with them. They were satisfied to observe, but they didn't participate, at least not at that moment.

The Jordan River symbolizes death in the Old Testament. Years before, when Joshua led God's people across the river, a similar event happened when the priests stepped into the water and "it piled up in a heap a great distance away, at a town called Adam" (Joshua 3:16). That's fascinating to me: This is a prophetic picture that someday Jesus, the second Adam, would come to break the curse of sin and death. The prophets loved God, and they knew the power of God, but they were unwilling to cross the river that symbolized the power of death. They didn't have a strong enough relationship with either of the two men to generate enough courage to follow them across the river.

After Elijah was taken up by the chariots of fire, these prophets had what they thought was a great idea: They wanted to send out a search party to look for Elijah. They thought he might be on a mountain or in a valley nearby! They badgered Elisha until he gave them permission to go, but of course, they didn't find him.

The two groups of prophets were near Elijah and Elisha, but they hung back without following too closely. Do you know people like that? Are you like that? There are many reasons for timidity, but if we hang back too much or too long, we miss the incredible blessing of being in a divine flow of meaningful connections with people.

SEVENTH, HOLD ON TO YOUR MOST IMPORTANT RELATIONSHIPS THROUGH ADVERSITY.

Why did Elisha follow his friend across the Jordan? Over the years, I've heard many preachers say it was because he wanted the double portion, but that's not what I see in the text. Elisha walked through the symbol of death with Elijah before the older man asked him what he wanted before he left the scene. I believe Elisha had the courage to cross the symbol of death simply because he loved his friend.

Elijah was the one who took the initiative to ask Elisha what he wanted. When Elisha answered, the older man told him, "You have asked a difficult thing, yet if you see me when I am taken from you, it will be yours—otherwise, it will not" (v. 10). Notice that he didn't say, "Fat chance!" and he didn't tell him, "That's so selfish!" But he also didn't make it easy. He was saying, "You've been with me a long time, and we've walked together through good times and bad. We get each other. You've asked for a lot, but God is a big God. If you'll stay with me to the end, He'll grant your request."

Elisha received the cloak of anointing and instantly saw two miracles: Elijah was raptured, and Elisha parted the Jordan just like his mentor had done only moments before. He then asked, "Where is the God of Elijah?" In other words, "God, will you come through for me like you did for him?"

Look for God's presence and power in your redemptive relationships. We live in time of social, economic, and political upheaval. It's easy to be discouraged, and it's just as easy to be resentful. We need to remember that God has given us a divine calling to reach the lost and make disciples wherever we go. I'm convinced this doesn't happen when we're isolated. Throughout history, the church has had the greatest impact when the body of believers loves each other and serves the community so that those who are watching have to say, "Those people have something I need!"

It's good to take stock of our relationships from time to time and ask, "God, where are You in these connections? I want to be in Your divine flow. Show me where You're leading me. Make me a blessing to the people You put in my life."

THE QUESTION

Who are you walking with today? I'm not suggesting that all God-appointed friendships are easy. Sometimes, they're challenging, but they're essential . . . for us and for our friends. I hope you're walking with people who see life from a different angle so you'll have better perception about yourself and what God has called you to be and do. Those people will expand your world and enrich your life.

I hope you'll connect with people God will use to encourage you deeply and help unlock your future so you can ask God for great things and He'll come through. The first step is to ask God to show you His divine flow and then agree to walk with the person(s) God puts next to you.

So . . . what's the essence of friendship? We could look at many different features of what makes a friendship strong, but in *The Four Loves*, C. S. Lewis clarifies what's essential:

> Friendship arises out of mere Companionship when two or more of the companions discover that they have in common some insight or interest or even taste which the others do not share and which, till that moment, each believed to be his own

unique treasure (or burden). The typical expression of opening Friendship would be something like, "What? You too? I thought I was the only one."

. . . It is when two such persons discover one another, when, whether with immense difficulties and semi-articulate fumblings or with what would seem to us amazing and elliptical speed, they share their vision —it is then that Friendship is born. [28]

Go and do likewise.

ME

14   FUJI RDP III

14

KING'S CAMP
MER ROUGE,
LOUISIANA
SUMMER 1996

THE LIONS AT E3 RANCH
FORT SCOTT, KANSAS
May 2020

I'M IN THE BACK ROW
SECOND FROM LEFT

consider
THIS

1

When was the last time you sensed a "divine flow" to connect with someone? What was the result?

....

....

....

....

....

....

....

2

Describe a relationship in your life that has seen some difficult moments but has been worth the effort to stay connected and go deeper. What was your cost-benefit analysis along the way? In other words, why did you stick it out?

....

....

....

....

....

....

....

3

What are some
differences between
"icky dependence"
and healthy
interdependence? Do
you have any experience
with the bad kind? If
so, what happened?

....

....

....

....

....

....

....

....

....

....

4

What excuses do
people use to stay
on the sidelines and
fail to move toward
friendships (or perhaps,
to be satisfied with
superficial friendships)?
Have you used any
of these excuses?
Explain your answer.

....

....

....

....

....

....

....

....

....

....

5

When you look at your
strongest friendships,
what are the factors
that cemented them?

....
....
....
....
....
....
....
....
....
....

6

Who are you walking
with today?

....
....
....
....
....
....
....
....
....
....

FIVE STAGES OF CONNECTION

1

STAGE 1

RELATE

WE WALK TOGETHER.

2

STAGE 2

TRUST

WE SHARE OUR STORIES.

3

STAGE 3

DISCLOSE

WE CONFESS OUR FAULTS
TO EACH OTHER.

4

STAGE 4

PROCESS

WE SUBMIT TO EACH OTHER.

5

STAGE 5

INTEGRATE

WE ACCEPT GOD'S GRACE.

CHAPTER EIGHT

TRUST

The second stage of building a great friendship is trust. At this point, people start telling their stories—not their deepest secrets, just the broad narrative of their lives. The way we tell our stories is just as important as the actual words. For instance, I have to work on positivity because I'm normally a glass-half-empty guy, but my daughter Sarah is just the opposite. She's the ultimate optimist. I can imagine taking her on a two-day trip when the first day was horrible but the second was terrific. When we get home and Amy asks, "How was your trip?" Sarah would say, "It was fantastic! We had a great time!" But I'd report, "It was a bummer. Nothing went right." Neither of us would be lying, yet neither of us told the whole story. It's the same way when you invite someone to "Tell me about yourself." Two people can go through the same event, but one comes out with more wisdom, humility, and compassion than before, while the other's heart is hardened in bitterness. The way they talk about the event tells us a lot about their perspective on life.

When we tell our stories, we leave out certain details and focus on others, we reveal our emotions (or the lack of them), and we give people a glimpse into our characters.

I remember talking to a man about his relationship with his wife. He told me in great detail that she had every reason to be unhappy with him because he wasn't creative or enthusiastic. He said, "I'm just a stick in the mud." As we talked, he used this self-descriptive phrase several times. I just listened and asked him to tell me more. At one point, I said, "Bro, I think I have a word from God for you." He looked surprised, but his body language told me to proceed. I said, "You're not a stick in the mud." That's all I said, but for him, it was plenty. He broke into tears. My comment wasn't the most emotion-packed statement I've ever heard or ever said, but God used it to tap into his shame and let him feel understood.

GLUE

Trust is the glue of any relationship. With it, we can overcome almost anything; without it, we feel helpless, hopeless, and alone. Some people trust others far too much and far too quickly, leaving themselves significantly exposed to harm, but the problem for many of us is just the opposite—we won't let anyone get below the surface. We're posers who don't want to admit we need anyone else, and if we don't need them, we don't develop interdependence . . . we don't lean on each other . . . we don't learn who and how to trust.

Sethry tells a story about working at the Belo Mansion in Dallas. Some years ago, the palatial private home was converted to an event center where the children of the super wealthy in the city get married and have blow-out parties. At the most lavish, expensive wedding reception he had ever seen (or even imagined), he was told to go to the kitchen where they needed help. As he went through the doors to the kitchen, he stepped from beauty and peace into chaos, flames, and cursing! A sous chef ran up to Sethry and a friend and yelled, "I need you two to cut some limes!" He took them to a table where "some limes" turned out to be two sacks full. The sous chef handed them knives that looked like machetes, and they started cutting. After a few minutes, Sethry noticed his friend was just standing there with a knife in one hand and a lime in the other. He wasn't moving. Sethry asked, "Hey, are you okay?"

"I . . . I cut myself," he moaned. He held his hand for Sethry to see, revealing a deep gash in his thumb.

At that moment the sous chef ran back to get the cut limes. He looked at Sethry's friend and demanded, "Why haven't you cut all the limes I gave you? Is anything wrong with you?"

TRUST IS THE GLUE OF ANY RELATIONSHIP. WITH IT, WE CAN OVERCOME ALMOST ANYTHING; WITHOUT IT, WE FEEL HELPLESS, HOPELESS & ALONE.

"No," he replied meekly. "I'm fine." As the sous chef glared at him, he again began cutting limes. With each stroke, more lime juice squirted into his open wound. He cut a few limes (which, of course, weren't usable since they had blood on them), but he hid the blood droplets from the staring eyes that were fixed on him. The sous chef finally got fed up with how slow the process was going, and he stormed away in a cloud of choice words. Sethry's friend took that opportunity to leave and have his hand stitched up.

One positive aspect of this story is that the friend trusted Sethry enough to reveal his wound and receive some comfort. But the friend responded to the sous chef the way many of us act when our bosses are looking . . . or our spouse is looking . . . or anyone under the sun is looking. We grimace at the pain we feel, but we insist, "I'm fine." We're very selective about who we trust . . . and for good reason.

If we think about the people we know, we can easily identify four types of trust:

✳ SOME PEOPLE TRUST BLINDLY.

They trust even untrustworthy people, including those who often lie to them, use them, and abuse them. They react to their sense that life isn't safe by trying to draw close to anybody— even those who have hurt them before and those who are likely to let them down.

✳ SOME PEOPLE REFUSE TO TRUST, AND THEY WITHDRAW.

They've come to the conclusion that they aren't safe, but their defense is to become invisible. They don't express opinions, they don't verbalize their desires, and they don't let anyone get too close. They may be in the room with other people, but they find some way to hide what's going on inside.

✳ SOME PEOPLE REFUSE TO TRUST, AND THEY INTIMIDATE.

These people have come to the same conclusion as those who withdraw— they're not safe—but their reaction is very different. They grit their teeth and tell themselves, "I'm never going to let anyone hurt me again! I'll make them afraid so they'll do anything I want them to do!"

*   AND SOME, MAYBE ONLY A FEW, HAVE LEARNED
       TO TRUST WISELY.

They trust only to the extent people have earned their trust, and they move forward with those who are willing to be open and honest. They speak the truth, but not to manipulate. They draw close, but not to control. This is where we want to go . . . this is where we need to go in our relationships. Is it even possible? Yes, thankfully, yes.

TRUST IS AN INVESTMENT

When people buy stocks, bonds, mutual funds, real estate, or any other investment, they calculate the risks. Successful investors come in all stripes, but they all have one thing in common: they're willing to take some risk—maybe not much, but at least a little. Shrewd choices by seasoned and effective investors were honed over years of trial and error. Gradually, they learned to spot companies where their money promised a good return.

We need to be like these wise money managers when we invest our trust in people. Probably through trial and error—or better, by watching others as they trust wisely or foolishly—we learn to spot people we're willing to move toward and take the risk of opening a window to our hearts.

When we think of people who have made what seemed to be really risky investments in relationships, it's easy to think of Jesus. Over and over in the Gospels, we see His closest followers misunderstand Him, and occasionally, we see them challenge Him. For instance, when Jesus told His disciples (again) that His purpose was to die for the sins of the world, Peter tried to correct him: "Never, Lord! This shall never happen to you!" Jesus said something that must have rocked Peter's world: "Get behind me, Satan! You are a stumbling block to me; you do not have in mind the concerns of God, but merely human concerns" (Matthew 16:22-23). Jesus was incredibly gracious to draw people close, but He was also willing to speak the truth when something needed to be said. Both of those behaviors elevate the level of trust in relationships.

When Jesus heard that His cousin, John the Baptist, had been beheaded by Herod, He got into a boat to find a place where He could be alone. The crowds who had heard about His miracles followed Him on foot, so when the boat reached shore, thousands of them were already there. Jesus, grieving but full of compassion, spent time with the people and healed the sick. As the sun went down, the disciples were worried because food trucks hadn't been invented yet and people were hungry. Jesus, as you know, took a boy's sack lunch and fed 5,000 men—probably a total closer to 20,000, including the women and children.

As soon as dinner was over, Jesus told the disciples to get into the boat and start rowing to the other side of the lake. He sent the crowd away, and He finally had a little time alone to think, pray, and grieve.

The guys in the boat, including several who were fishermen, weren't making much progress in the night voyage because a strong wind was against them. Let's pick up the story with Matthew's account:

> Shortly before dawn Jesus went out to them, walking on the lake. When the disciples saw him walking on the lake, they were terrified. "It's a ghost," they said, and cried out in fear.

But Jesus immediately said to them: "Take courage! It is I. Don't be afraid."

"Lord, if it's you," Peter replied, "tell me to come to you on the water."

"Come," he said.

Then Peter got down out of the boat, walked on the water and came toward Jesus. (Matthew 14:25-29)

We usually focus on what comes next: Peter began to doubt, and he sank like a rock. He called out to Jesus, and He reached out to take Peter's hand to bring him up. This, Matthew tells us, was more impressive to the disciples than even the miracle with the bread and fish that happened only hours before. They were amazed and told Him, "Truly you are the Son of God" (v. 33).

But I want to go back to the moment in the boat when the disciples were in trouble and they saw Jesus. In Mark's Gospel, which many scholars believe was his recording of Peter's story, he tells us that Jesus "intended to go past them" (Mark 6:48). Get this: the disciples were straining to make progress on the sea at night in a high wind. They looked over and noticed Jesus walking by them. At first, they wondered if they were in season four of *Stranger Things*, but He assured them they weren't looking at a ghost—it really was Jesus. I can imagine Jesus nodding and saying, "How's it going, guys?" If they were like many of us, they would have said, "We're fine. It's a little rough, but we'll make it. See you later." Jesus wasn't out there on a rescue mission. He was just walking by.

But at that moment, something in Peter changed. He wasn't willing to just let things play out and meet Jesus on the shore in a few hours. He didn't want to settle for survival, for the run of the mill, for watching Jesus walk past them. He called out, "Lord, if it's you, tell me to come to you on the water." (That's hilarious. Who else would it be?) He was asking, "Jesus, can

I trust You? Are You really there for me? Can I do something I've never dreamed of doing and still be safe?"

Jesus responded to Peter's fledgling trust with a bold assurance that it was worth the risk. He replied simply, "Come." Peter had been following Jesus for a while. They had been relating, walking miles from town to town, talking, enjoying meals, and camping out. Now, they moved to the second stage in meaningful relationships: trust. Peter could have remained in the boat on that stormy night, but he didn't settle for staying safe. He wanted more—more of Jesus and more of the life He offered. Jesus didn't command Peter to get out and walk on the water, but Peter chose to make an investment in his relationship with Jesus, and we read about it today. In *The Inner Circle*, novelist Brad Meltzer has the narrator observe: "In this world, there was nothing scarier than trusting someone. But there was also nothing more rewarding." [29] Peter was richly rewarded for trusting Jesus that night.

Trust is a courageous choice. We can come up with a dozen reasons why we prefer to remain safe behind a wall of distrust, but when we do, we miss out on life's greatest adventures and biggest rewards. Some people, especially men who want to project a tough exterior, believe trust and vulnerability are signs of weakness. They're not. In fact, they're perhaps the clearest indication of security and confidence.

On the other side, some of us need a large dose of courage to speak the truth about an untrustworthy person. Trust isn't the goal . . . *trusting wisely* is the goal. This isn't an excuse to stay behind walls and erect machine gun turrets, but some of us have foolishly trusted people who have abused us, abandoned us, and used us for their selfish ends.

Choose trust, but choose to trust trustworthy people, those who have a track record of integrity, honesty, and care for others. I'm certainly not suggesting we need to find perfect people—there was only one of them—but we need to look for people who are trustworthy enough.

And we need to be people who are worthy of people trusting us with their hearts. Are we willing and able to listen, care, and be patient with a process? Do we speak the truth in love? The truth without love brutalizes people, and love without truth is sentimental mush. We need to hold truth in one hand and love in the other, using both to hold the hearts of the people close to us.

Peter didn't walk on water that night because he was looking for a thrill. He stepped out of the boat because Jesus had proven himself to be trustworthy. Peter's level of trust was just barely enough to get him to step out, but it was enough. And when his trust failed and he began to sink, Jesus again proved himself by reaching out and taking his hand.

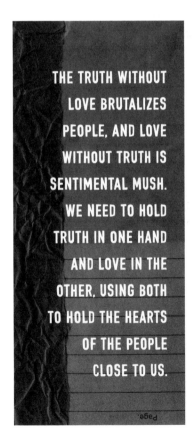

THE TRUTH WITHOUT LOVE BRUTALIZES PEOPLE, AND LOVE WITHOUT TRUTH IS SENTIMENTAL MUSH. WE NEED TO HOLD TRUTH IN ONE HAND AND LOVE IN THE OTHER, USING BOTH TO HOLD THE HEARTS OF THE PEOPLE CLOSE TO US.

Jesus didn't push himself on Peter that night. He didn't say, "Hey, I know more than you, and you're incompetent without Me." It may have been true, but Jesus, the consummate gentleman, waited for Peter to voice his request. We often criticize Peter for his wavering faith that caused him to sink, but he was the only one who got out of the boat. Jesus is, as always, the hero of the story, but in my eyes, Peter comes in second.

TELL YOUR STORY

Peter and Jesus had walked together, and they undoubtedly had told many personal stories on the road and around campfires. (I wonder if Jesus said, "Yeah, I remember the day I started creating the universe.") But on this windy night, Peter was telling more of the story of his heart. He wanted more than safety. He wanted more than the status quo. He wanted more, and He was eager to trust his friend and take a big chance to connect with Him on a deeper level.

When you tell your story, is it a novel or a memoir? Do you fictionalize the facts to make yourself look better? (In case you're wondering, the answer is "Yes!" We all do, at least some of the time.) We're wary of politicians and journalists who "spin" the facts to suit their interests, but don't we do the same thing? I'm not recommending that you spill your guts to anyone and everyone. Be wise, be selective, be discreet, but find somebody who has proven to honor the truth in other people's lives, and tell at least one truth about yourself that isn't spun. You don't need to tell everything all at once. That's not a good idea. Share a single fact and a feeling, and see how it's received. If you feel comfortable, share more the next time, and the next.

Some of us assume our story is so boring that it isn't worth telling. Let me assure you, that's baloney. We may not know how to tell it very well, but each of us is created in the image of God, and we've been rescued out of darkness and transferred into God's marvelous light by the death and resurrection of Jesus. We all love adventure stories, and each of us has our own dramatic story of being plucked from danger. Your story is a gift to the people who love you. They need to know what makes you tick, they need to understand the past events that have shaped your present responses, and they delight in hearing stories of rescue and reconciliation.

People learn life's most important lessons from our stories, and we learn from theirs. At the end of the account of Jesus and Peter walking on the water, all the disciples had the same response: they were convinced that Jesus was truly the Son of God. Eleven of them stayed safe in the boat, but Peter's courageous trust made a difference in their lives, too. Courageous steps of trust in one relationship benefit others. (Can you imagine their conversation when Peter got back in the boat? I wish I could have been there!)

Are you able to hear someone's honest memoir without condemning the person, zoning out because you're bored, or jumping in to fix the person's problems? Those responses are red flags that we're not yet completely trustworthy, and we need to heal and grow so we can handle the truth people share with us.

Let me give you a listener's pro tip. Whenever you listen to people, the very best response—the one that communicates love and values truth—is the sincere invitation, "Tell me more about that." Try it. It's pure gold.

A FEW GOOD QUESTIONS

As you think about connecting with people and inviting them to tell their story, let me offer a few questions you can ask:

* *"HOW ARE YOU DOING . . . REALLY?"*

✳ *"WHAT IS A HIGH AND A LOW IN YOUR LIFE RIGHT NOW?"*

✳ *"WOULD YOU TELL ME MORE OF YOUR STORY?"*

✳ *"HOW ARE THINGS GOING IN YOUR MOST IMPORTANT RELATIONSHIPS (WITH YOUR SPOUSE + KIDS + PARENTS + FRIENDS + COWORKERS)?"*

✳ *"HOW'S YOUR RELATIONSHIP WITH GOD? WHAT'S ENCOURAGING TO YOU? WHAT'S CONFUSING OR DISCOURAGING?"*

Asking questions like these isn't a timed test, and people don't get extra credit for finishing early. You may not get beyond the first one, but that's perfectly fine. The questions are only tools to help you achieve the real goal: to get to know people at a deeper level. Try these with your spouse and your kids, or if you're single, with your two or three best friends. Be a great listener, and sprinkle in "Tell me more about that." You might be amazed at what you hear. And when it's appropriate, share a bit of your story. If the person asks for more, take the next step in being a little more open.

NEVER OFF LIMITS

The "one another" passages in the New Testament tell us that meaningful, supportive connections are essential in the body of Christ. Small groups are often the place where people feel safe enough to be real with their hopes and fears. In these groups, life change happens through a process of growth with people who trust each other, or more likely, are learning to trust each other. But even in the business world, experts realize the importance of trust in building effective teams. In an article in *Harvard Business Review*, Emma Seppälä explains that vulnerability is high on the list of necessary traits for executives:

Why do we feel more comfortable around someone who is authentic and vulnerable? Because we are particularly sensitive to signs of trustworthiness in our leaders. Servant leadership, for example, which is characterized by authenticity and values-based leadership, yields more positive and constructive behavior in employees and greater feelings of hope and trust in both the leader and the organization. In turn, trust in a leader improves employee performance. You can even see this at the level of the brain. Employees who recall a boss who resonated with them show enhanced activation in parts of the brain related to positive emotion and social connection. The reverse is true when they think of a boss who did not resonate. [30]

As we saw at the beginning of this book, we're created to connect. We long for rich, real relationships with God and with at least a few people. In fact, we can't thrive without them. Actress Celeste Holm spoke the truth when she said, "We live by encouragement and die without it—slowly, sadly and angrily."

Love, joy, forgiveness, and encouragement never happen when we're alone; they only happen in relationships . . . but of course, not in every relationship, or even in many of them. They happen only when two people have found each other to be trustworthy. There's always a measure of risk when we choose to trust, and even the most trustworthy people are flawed and let us down sometimes—just as we let them down at times. So, is it worth it? Are the potential benefits greater than our fears of what might happen?

For me, the answer is "Yes!" In fact, I'll do just about anything, and pay any price, to develop deeper, more vulnerable, very honest relationships with Amy, my children (and now my grandson), and with the men I walk with every day.

SARAH + FRIENDS PRAYING AT GRADUATION
JULY 2020

ZACH C.
ME
ZACH S
ANDREW
SETHRY

↓

KING'S CAMP
REUNION
OCTOBER 2020

consider THIS

1

How have you seen trust violated? How did those experiences (either yours or others' as you observed them) affect your willingness and ability to form good relationships?

....

....

....

....

....

....

....

2

What are some ways you can tell if someone is trustworthy? Who are the people who fit these criteria in your life? Describe the benefits of your relationship with them.

....

....

....

....

....

....

....

3

When you tell your story,
is it a novel or a memoir?
Explain your answer.

....

....

....

....

....

....

....

....

....

....

4

When is it wise to
trust someone?
When is it foolish?

....

....

....

....

....

....

....

....

....

5

When was the last time
you listened to someone
and you said at some
point, "Tell me more
about that"? Why is this
statement pure gold?

....
....
....
....
....
....
....
....
....

6

How would asking "a
few good questions"
help you connect
with people on a
deeper level?

....
....
....
....
....
....
....
....
....

Five Stages of Connection

1

STAGE 1

RELATE

WE WALK TOGETHER.

2

STAGE 2

TRUST

WE SHARE OUR STORIES.

3

STAGE 3

DISCLOSE

WE CONFESS OUR FAULTS
TO EACH OTHER.

4

STAGE 4

PROCESS

WE SUBMIT TO EACH OTHER.

5

STAGE 5

INTEGRATE

WE ACCEPT GOD'S GRACE.

CHAPTER NINE

DISCLOSE

When we relate, we're just hanging out with no pressure and limited expectations. As we get to know each other, we learn who and how to trust. As the relationship grows deeper and stronger, we feel permission to be increasingly open and disclose more of ourselves. Here, in the third stage, we feel safe enough to start asking each other hard questions. A few years ago, I must have done something really dumb because Amy sincerely asked me, "Jonathan, are you being stupid on purpose?" Her question wasn't whether I was being stupid (apparently that part was obvious), only whether I intended to be. Thanks, Honey.

When we disclose, we're revealing the parts of our stories we haven't wanted anyone to know about. We're in control, so we can limit how much we tell, and to whom. There's no pressure and no timetable, but this is the stage when we take the risk to trust someone more fully, with the expectation of feeling more known and loved than ever before. We may relate and trust in a group, but from this stage on, it's entirely one-on-one.

Let's be realistic: It's hard enough for a staff team, a volunteer team, a small group at a church, or a couple to move past Stage 2 and begin to disclose one-on-one—and we have the resources of truth, the power of the Spirit,

> **WE MAY RELATE & TRUST IN A GROUP. BUT FROM THIS STAGE ON. IT'S ENTIRELY ONE-ON-ONE.**

and the love of God! In the business world, the only way to advance past Stage 2 is to have a mentor or coach relationship with one or more people on the team. And even then, it's important to move very slowly and carefully. On these teams, knowing others' stories provides plenty of understanding, which is the grease that helps the engine run more smoothly. Go with that.

SOURCES OF STRESS

Most of us have become accustomed to quite a bit of stress. I've heard people compare our lives with pressure cookers. If we don't have a release valve, the pressure can build until we explode . . . and that's not a pretty sight. The explosion may take the form of outbursts of anger, but it can also result in implosions of depression. For many people, it's both. When we recall hurts that have been hidden and disclose events that have discolored our lives with toxic shame, we let out some steam and the pressure subsides. But once isn't enough. We face all kinds of stresses, and even positive and pleasant activities (such as weddings, graduations, vacations, and birthdays) add to our stress. We need at least a few relationships with people who help us let off steam by hearing us talk about our hurts and flaws.

Some people have the emotional capacity to handle a lot of stress, but most of us don't. Even for those who can take a lot of pressure, a tipping point comes sooner or later. Years ago, a study was conducted to determine the impact of various events. Each event was given a score compared to getting married, which was assigned the score of 50. Researchers found that the value of each event was remarkably similar across race, gender, age, and culture. It's no surprise that painful events scored highest. For instance:

DEATH OF A SPOUSE	100
DIVORCE	73
DEATH OF A CLOSE FAMILY MEMBER	63
DETENTION IN JAIL	63
MAJOR INJURY OR ILLNESS	53
BEING FIRED	47

But positive events can also raise the level of stress:

MARITAL RECONCILIATION	45
RETIREMENT	45
PREGNANCY	40
CLOSING A MORTGAGE ON A NEW HOME	31
SON OR DAUGHTER LEAVING HOME	29
OUTSTANDING PERSONAL ACHIEVEMENT	28

Of course, an individual may experience several of these events within a short period of time, adding to the cumulative total. When we don't have a way to relieve the pressure, each new event, painful or pleasant, raises the pressure in the pot.[31]

THE POWER OF CONFESSION

Yeah, I know. The mere mention of *confession* has made some of you get sweaty palms. Confession is generally seen as something to be avoided at all costs. We don't want to expose ourselves, and we don't want to be condemned. I get that, but that's why we postpone it during the first two stages. We feel far more confident and comfortable disclosing our flaws to someone we trust—in fact, we shouldn't disclose them to anyone we don't trust. That would be naïve and harmful.

Confession, as we've seen, means to agree with. If we've sinned, we agree with God that what we did or said was wrong, and we agree that He has already forgiven us because Jesus paid the full price for all sins on the cross. We can also confess that we're burdened, confused, angry, afraid, stressed, and burned out. These sensations aren't necessarily sins, but if we don't find the release valve, they can create emotional, relational, and physical damage. But we also confess the truth about God. Paul wrote to the Romans, "If you confess with your mouth the Lord Jesus and believe in your heart that God has raised Him from the dead, you will be saved" (Romans 10:9 NKJV). All three types of confession—of sin, of forgiveness, and of stress—are crucial if we want to walk in freedom and joy.

In the stage of disclosure, we'll probably notice patterns in our confessions—and these patterns give us far more insight into the recesses of our hearts. I have some friends who have attended Alcoholics Anonymous, and they tell me the turning point for the people in the program is in Steps 4 and 5:

* IN STEP 4, PEOPLE MAKE "A SEARCHING AND FEARLESS MORAL INVENTORY" OF THEIR LIVES.

They examine not only their destructive behavior and its effects, but also their patterns of thinking, believing, feeling, and acting. They look at their history and every relationship, every goal, every success, and every failure. This step is, from all I've heard, a grueling but necessary process, and at the end, people have far better understanding of how they arrived at their current condition. But that's not the most challenging step.

* IN STEP 5, THEY ADMIT "TO GOD, TO OURSELVES, AND TO ANOTHER HUMAN BEING THE EXACT NATURE OF OUR WRONGS."

It's one thing to write out all the messes of your life when you're alone, but it's quite another to look someone in the eye and verbalize what you've tried to hide for many years. Many people report that this is the most difficult thing they've ever done, but also the most freeing. When we tell another person what's really going on, we're vulnerable. The power of AA, and even more, the power of a healthy body of Christ, is that when people are vulnerable, no one sneers or laughs. The only response is love and the assurance of God's forgiveness.

Author Ann Voscamp is on target when she writes, "Shame dies where stories are told in safe places. Shame poisons hope—poisons the hope that things can change. That we can ever be changed, ever be accepted, ever be good enough."[32] Disclosure brings the causes of shame into the light of God's love, forgiveness, and acceptance . . . and God's light is stronger than shame.

SHAME DIES WHERE STORIES ARE TOLD IN SAFE PLACES.

– ANN VOSCAMP –

Ironically, confession has the power to either crush or restore. People can confess in two very different ways. Some try to use self-condemnation as a sign they're not so bad after all. They call them-selves terrible names and wallow in shame to prove they're truly repentant. This type of "confession" is really self-pity, and it isn't a productive lifestyle! It leaves us more self-absorbed, more anxious about the next sin, and more afraid to let anyone know what's going on with us.

But effective confession begins with the assurance of God's great mercy and compassion. Through confession, we reconnect to His limitless source of love and forgiveness. Are we grieved that we've sinned? Yes, but our grief soon gives way to the joy of God's delight in us, the relief of knowing we've been cleansed of all sin, and a fresh commitment to please the One who loves us so much.

Do you see the difference? Sadly, the self-pity form of confession is all too common in the church. It's another "work" to earn God's love. I believe God is calling us to trust in His grace, not only to go to heaven when we die, but to live each day in the wonder of His love.

WHOSE INITIATIVE?

We usually assume that we take the lead in confession. We feel the burden of sin, we feel the stress of life, and we choose to thank God for what He has given us. But in a very poignant passage of Scripture, we see Jesus taking the initiative to restore someone who had really messed up.

I think it's very hard for us to imagine the incredibly high expectations among the disciples at the Last Supper. Jesus had ridden into Jerusalem the Sunday before with the crowds yelling, "Hosanna to the King!" During the week, He had gone to the temple almost every day. The religious leaders tried to catch Him in a false statement, but He made them look like angry schoolboys. At the dinner, the disciples were excited . . . for all the wrong reasons. They were sure Jesus was about to be inaugurated as the King, and they were jockeying for positions in His cabinet. Imagine the scene: Jesus faced abandonment, betrayal, torture, and death, and the disciples were picking out the rugs for their new offices.

Again, Jesus told them He was going to be killed, but they misunderstood (again) because He said it would bring Him glory. How could His death be glorious? They had no idea. Then He told them He was going away. That must have been really confusing. But since relationships were always at the top of His mind and in the center of His heart, He told them, "A new command I give you: Love one another. As I have loved you, so you must love one another. By this everyone will know that you are my disciples, if you love one another."

Peter wasn't paying attention to this last part. He was still fixed on Jesus' previous statement. He asked, "Lord, where are you going?"

Jesus tried to assure him, "Where I am going, you cannot follow now, but you will follow later."

Peter was confused: "Lord, why can't I follow you now?" Then, to be sure everybody knew the depth of his devotion, he told Jesus: "I will lay down my life for you."

Jesus probably grimaced and smiled at the same time when He replied, "Will you really lay down your life for me? Very truly I tell you, before the rooster crows, you will disown me three times!" (John 13:31-38)

Only hours later, after a long walk and talk with the disciples, Jesus was betrayed by Judas and arrested by soldiers and men who represented the Pharisees. They led Him to the high priest, and Peter followed along behind. As Peter stood near a fire to keep warm, a servant girl questioned if he was a follower of Jesus. He denied it. Later, a group of people asked the same question, and he denied it again. And finally, a relative of Malchus, the man whose ear Peter had cut off during a scuffle at the arrest, asked, "Didn't I see you with him in the garden?" For the third time, Peter denied Jesus, and a rooster crowed (John 18:15-27).

At that moment, Jesus turned from the soldiers beating Him and looked at Peter. A wave of shame overwhelmed the guilt-ridden disciple. He had failed the one who loved him. He had denied even knowing Him. Peter hadn't denied Jesus because a Roman soldier had threatened his life; he denied Him to a servant girl, some strangers, and a guy who wasn't even sure he could identify him. Luke tells us, "And he went outside and wept bitterly" (Luke 22:60-62).

Thankfully, that's not the end of the story for Peter, even though I'm sure he thought it was. On Sunday morning, an angel appeared to the women at the tomb to announce the incredible news that Jesus had been raised from the dead! He told them, "But go, tell his disciples and Peter, 'He is going ahead of you into Galilee. There you will see him, just as he told you'" (Mark 16:7). Peter had denied Jesus, but Jesus hadn't given up on him.

Jesus appeared to the disciples several times after His resurrection, but one was surely the most striking for Peter. He and a few other disciples had gone fishing at the Sea of Galilee. They fished all night, but their nets were empty. In the dawn's light, they saw a man on the beach. He yelled to ask if they'd caught any fish, and they told him, "No." He told them, "Throw your net on the right side of the boat and you will find some." Suddenly, their net was full of fat fish!

Peter realized the man was Jesus. In his excitement, he put on his clothes, jumped in the water, and swam to shore. Jesus had prepared a breakfast of fish and bread over an open fire.

The word John used for the fire that morning indicated a *charcoal* fire, the same kind that Peter stood beside when he was warming himself the night he denied Jesus. Smell is one of the most powerful triggers of memory, and John's careful use of the words leads us to the conclusion that Jesus had carefully orchestrated this moment. Jesus was reminding Peter of his worst sin—not to shame him, but to restore him.

After breakfast, Jesus took Peter aside and asked him three times: "Simon, son of John, do you love me?" Each time, I'm sure Peter's heart was flooded with intense emotions. Jesus knew that the level of Peter's restoration was dependent on the level of honesty about his sins. He used a charcoal fire to remind Peter of the actual events, He took him aside so he wouldn't be embarrassed in front of his friends, and He gave him the same number of opportunities to express his devotion as he had denied Him.

Then, Jesus told him his restoration was so complete that he would die a death that was much like His own: "Very truly I tell you, when you were younger you dressed yourself and went where you wanted; but when you are old you will stretch out your hands, and someone else will dress you and lead you where you do not want to go." And Jesus repeated the invitation He had given so many times before: "Follow me" (John 21:1-19).

Jesus, in His incredible kindness, didn't wait with His arms folded for Peter to muster the courage to come to Him. Instead, on Easter morning He gave specific instructions through the angel not to leave Peter out, and later He crafted a beautiful moment on the beach to fully restore him.

If Jesus had treated Peter like sinners are treated in many of our churches (and on many of our staff teams), the scene of Peter weeping bitterly would be the last we'd have seen of him. But Jesus forgave before Peter repented, and Jesus took the initiative to engage with Peter when he probably wanted to crawl into a hole and die.

This is a picture of what we need when we disclose our hearts to someone we trust, and this is a picture of how to treat people who have royally messed up their lives . . . and those who haven't, but feel like they have.

The rest of the story is found in Luke's history of the early church. Peter became the chief spokesman and leader of God's purpose to plant the church in Jerusalem and see it expand to every corner of the globe. Restoration only comes through honest confession, but when it comes, it's amazing!

WHO QUALIFIES?

In Chapter 3, we looked at the story of Simon of Cyrene, the man who picked up and carried Jesus' cross when He was too weak to carry it. Simon was willing to bear Jesus' burden. Simon's name means "listener," and we concluded that one of the main ways we can carry another person's burden is to listen intently to their stories. Being a listener as people disclose their hopes and fears and confess their faults is a high honor and a great responsibility. Sometimes, this step requires us to give notice of the limits of confidentiality (the ones we addressed in Chapter 3), with clear communication and sensitivity to the person's level of emotional distress.

Many people fear the consequences of their honesty, such as being fired or enduring others' gossiping. But when someone reveals a deep wound or significant wrong to the right person, confession brings restoration, which produces safety and stability. The one who shares with honesty and courage is no longer alone, so there's more support and wisdom than ever before.

Some prefer the added safety of disclosing secrets only to a professional counselor. I recommend competent counselors all the time, but at some point, I recommend that the people who see counselors also begin to share with others—personally, gradually, and appropriately—so we can add our love and support. If we're serious about living New Testament lives, we'll find ways to love one another, accept one another, forgive one another, rebuke one another, and encourage one another.

A dear friend of mine warns, "Beware of wasted vulnerability." This can happen when we share with someone who may be willing to hear at a surface level, but not at deeper levels. Quite often, we find out too late that we've said more than we should have. Or if we're the listeners, we need to count the costs of being involved at a deeper level with someone. It's perfectly fine to use a pastoral counseling model, listening for three or four times and then referring to a professional, but if that's your plan, be sure to explain this limitation early in the conversation.

BEWARE OF WASTED VULNERABILITY.

The stage of disclosure is a turning point, certainly for the one who is speaking, but also for the listener. Deep friendships are formed, hope is rekindled, walls are broken down, hearts are mended, and forgiveness is assured. Sounds pretty good, doesn't it?

1

Does reading this chapter terrify you or excite you? Explain your response.

....

....

....

....

....

....

....

2

How would you describe the level of stress you're experiencing in your life right now? Do you have a release valve on your pressure cooker? If not, what would it look like? If you do, what can you do for it to work more effectively?

....

....

....

....

....

....

....

3

For you, does confession typically result in feelings of self-pity and shame, or relief and thankfulness? Explain your answer.

....

....

....

....

....

....

....

....

....

4

How do you imagine Peter felt, and what do you think was going on in his mind at the breakfast and the conversation with Jesus on the beach?

....

....

....

....

....

....

....

....

....

....

5

Who in your life
is qualified to be
a listener as you
disclose your flaws?
Are you qualified?
Why or why not?

....

....

....

....

....

....

....

....

....

....

....

....

....

....

....

....

....

....

....

....

Five Stages of Connection

1

STAGE 1

RELATE

WE WALK TOGETHER.

2

STAGE 2

TRUST

WE SHARE OUR STORIES.

3

STAGE 3

DISCLOSE

WE CONFESS OUR FAULTS
TO EACH OTHER.

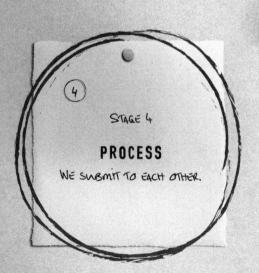

4

STAGE 4

PROCESS

WE SUBMIT TO EACH OTHER.

5

STAGE 5

INTEGRATE

WE ACCEPT GOD'S GRACE.

CHAPTER TEN

PROCESS

When we invite people to disclose their secrets and long-buried emotions to us (always one-on-one), the purpose isn't only to gather information. It's that, but it's much more than that. At that moment, we hold their hearts in our hands, and they trust us to be kind, gentle, and firm.

To help others process the lies they've believed, the assumptions that are based on those lies, the pains and losses that have never been grieved, and the healing that comes from honesty, we need to have gone through this process ourselves. We must be, as Henri Nouwen, said, "wounded healers." In his book by that title, he asserts, "The great illusion of leadership is to think that man can be led out of the desert by someone who has never been there." And as we listen to people reveal what's in their hearts, we see our own hurt, fear, and anger more clearly. Nouwen explains:

> Through compassion it is possible to recognize that the craving for love that people feel resides also in our own hearts, that the cruelty the world knows all too well is also rooted in our own impulses. Through compassion we also sense our hope for forgiveness in our friends' eyes and our hatred in their bitter mouths. When they

kill, we know that we could have done it; when they give life, we know that we can do the same. For a compassionate person nothing human is alien: no joy and no sorrow, no way of living and no way of dying. [33]

In the processing stage, the universe of people who are both willing and capable continues to shrink. Why? Because most people have never been in a safe relationship with someone who invited them to take the step to disclose what's really going on inside, much less someone who has the compassion, skill, and patience to help them process their false beliefs and painful emotions. The first three stages—relate, trust, and disclose—are intuitive for most of us, but processing requires some prophetic qualities, so we need maturity and training. Making the right connection at this stage is essential. If it's possible to "waste vulnerability" in the stage of disclosure on people who aren't ready or able to hear what's at the heart of our stories, we certainly don't want to be foolish in picking the wrong person to help us process our pain.

The goal of processing is facilitating a shift away from "perception management" as a primary focus and a move toward greater levels of authenticity, freedom, and emotional health. As we've seen before, we're very protective of our public image, and we tend to carefully craft it so we look wise, cool, handsome or beautiful, smart, and totally put together. But in this stage, we stop posing, starting in our conversations with one person. That's all it takes: just one person who will help us resolve inner conflicts, face our sorrows, take steps out of the quagmire, and experience renewed hope and courage. People may need to process how they've suffered abuse or abandonment, they may need to deal with an addiction, or they may have harmed someone and kept it a secret until now. As I've mentioned, I would rather our team be healthy than scandal-free. If we provide a safe enough environment, we'll hear some things that are awkward and uncomfortable. That's not only okay with me; I see it as a sign of healthy, God-honoring trust in relationships.

In the Gospels, we see people who were so eager to connect with Jesus that they didn't care about their reputations. When Jesus approached Jericho, blind Bartimaeus shouted, "Jesus, Son of David, have mercy on me!" The people around him told him to be quiet. They were embarrassed that he was making such a racket, but he wasn't. He kept shouting, "Son of David, have mercy on me!" And Jesus brought him close and gave him sight (Mark 10:46-52).

In another encounter, when Jesus and His disciples returned to Capernaum from across the lake, a man was waiting anxiously for Him. Jairus was a synagogue official, a role that combined civil and spiritual responsibilities. He was probably the leading citizen in the community. His daughter was dying, and his desperation to help her shattered any desire to be seen as distinguished and in control. He "came and fell at Jesus' feet, pleading with him to come to his house because his only daughter, a girl of about twelve, was dying." On the way to Jairus's home, a large crowd followed them, and a sick woman reached out to touch Jesus' cloak and was healed. She expected to remain anonymous, but Jesus stopped the speeding EMS truck to

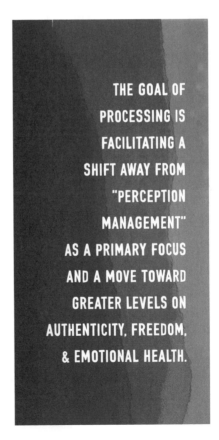

THE GOAL OF PROCESSING IS FACILITATING A SHIFT AWAY FROM "PERCEPTION MANAGEMENT" AS A PRIMARY FOCUS AND A MOVE TOWARD GREATER LEVELS ON AUTHENTICITY, FREEDOM, & EMOTIONAL HEALTH.

identify her and connect personally with her. When He finally turned to go to see the little girl, Jairus had already gotten word that she had died. At that moment, it appeared that Jairus's reputation might be shattered because he had trusted in Jesus, but He didn't come through. And Jesus' reputation might have been equally shattered because He had failed to help a local official. Yet Jesus told Jairus to look past his grief and have hope. The group arrived at his house, and Jesus raised the little girl from the dead (Luke 8:40-56).

Jairus twice took risks to be completely vulnerable: first when Jesus got out of the boat, and later after He had taken the time to help someone else. Because Jairus cared more for his daughter than his reputation, he saw Jesus do the impossible.

NO HURRY

The stages outlined in these chapters aren't a rigid program with deadlines and specific outcomes. This isn't engineering; it's messy humanity. Whether you're on the giving end or the receiving end, don't rush the process. No one is on the clock. Wrestling with life's deepest problems is never a straight line to success. When grief counselors describe the stages of dealing with death and other losses, they explain that people regularly lurch forward and slide backward to an earlier stage. The anger they finally let themselves feel may be so unnerving that they go back to trying to figure out what they can do to avoid the uncomfortable feelings.

We've already seen that you don't owe the other person anything. It's not a transactional relationship. If anyone wants to slow down, or even put the brakes on for a while, that's perfectly fine. No harm, no foul.

Sometimes, when people have disclosed quite a bit, they want to press on into the process stage and pursue resolution, but others have a very different reaction: they feel emotionally spent, and they want to go back to relating at Topgolf for weeks if not months. If this happens, don't assume the person is a coward, and don't push at all. Give time and space for the Spirit to work His will in His way in His timing. When the person has emotionally regrouped, the process stage may look less daunting.

Some might object: "Jonathan, this sounds like it'll take way too much time . . . time we need to be working to expand the kingdom." Honestly, I don't think it takes much additional time at all. Our connections with family, teams, and friends are already there. We just need to devote our time with them to an added purpose of establishing deeper relational connections. And actually, as people are freed from the crushing weight of their past, they become more focused, more optimistic, and more enthused to make a difference. Getting to that point takes some time and attention, but I'm talking about months in most cases, not decades.

DEEP WATERS

The stage of processing a person's broken heart is described in many places in the Scriptures. For instance, Solomon noted, "The purposes of a person's heart are deep waters, but one who has insight draws them out" (Proverbs 20:5). Below a certain depth in the oceans, light doesn't penetrate, but scientists have developed submarines that can withstand the enormous pressure to dive as far as seven miles beneath the surface. On these dives, they've seen incredible creatures, some that are luminescent, and they have solved a number of mysteries. When people invite us to dive deep and explore the mysteries of their hearts, we can help them discover truths they haven't seen before.

Sometimes, those who are new in the role of mentoring have an exaggerated view of their abilities and power, and they want to be the hero in the relationship, but those who are more experienced have learned that people thrive when they get input from several different sources. Solomon applied this principle to nations, but it also applies to individuals: "For lack of guidance a nation falls, but victory is won through many advisers" (Proverbs 11:14). No one has a monopoly on helping people grow.

Today, our society is incredibly polarized. Both sides are absolutely sure they're right—and they're convinced the other side is evil and stupid! I hate to say this, but the Bible describes these people as fools. More than ever, our thoughts are shaped by "confirmation bias," which means we hear only what we want to hear, and we discount anything that challenges our perspective. But Solomon had a very different suggestion: "The way of fools seems right to them, but the wise listen to advice" (Proverbs 12:15). Many of us have been foolish far too long, not just about politics, but more importantly, when we've been unwilling to listen to advice about the condition of our hearts from people who are wise, loving, and kind. Isolation eventually and inevitably makes us stupid. Left to ourselves, we can easily rationalize almost any behavior, but in the light of another person's observation, we're faced with the truth—the hard truth of our flaws and the glorious truth of God's grace.

> ISOLATION EVENTUALLY AND INEVITABLY MAKES US STUPID.

Processing is the riskiest stage, and it's the most uncomfortable because we look at the *why*, not just the *what*, but it's also the most rewarding part of the journey—for both the one diving into the deep end of the pool for the first time and the lifeguard who makes sure that person doesn't drown.

Find someone who treats your heart like a treasure, even if it needs some cleaning. And never, ever disclose your heart to anyone who has a track record of weaponizing anyone's vulnerability. If someone demands that you trust him, that's a red flag...a huge red flag.

NOT SO FAST!

Am I saying no one is qualified? Not exactly, but that's not a bad assumption at first. Certainly, if we look carefully, we can find counselors who are trained for this purpose, and even other believers who have experienced the power of genuine "one another" relationships and are equipped to help others process distorted thoughts and powerful emotions. But we do need to choose wisely.

One of the most famous people in the Bible had friends who appeared compassionate at first, but soon became toxic. I'm talking about Job. You know the story: he suffered calamity after calamity. A raiding party captured oxen and donkeys and killed his servants. Lightning struck his livestock and servants, incinerating them. Another group of raiders stole his camels and killed those who were looking after them. Then, a violent storm struck the house where his sons and daughters were staying, and all were killed. None of this was expected; Job was crushed. Still, he clung to his faith in God:

> "Naked I came from my mother's womb,
>> and naked I will depart.
> The LORD gave and the LORD has taken away;
>> may the name of the LORD be praised." (Job 1:21)

Job's trials, though, weren't over. In his grief, he was afflicted with boils all over his body. These weren't pimples, they were deep, painful infections. His wife's response was somewhat less than encouraging: "Are you still maintaining your integrity for nothing? Curse God and die!" (Job 2:9) Thanks, Sweetheart. I appreciate your help.

In the story, we see some things the friends did right, and of course, some things they did wrong.

 WHAT THEY DID RIGHT

Three of Job's friends heard about his tragic loss, and they responded with compassionate care:

> When Job's three friends, Eliphaz the Temanite, Bildad the Shuhite and Zophar the Naamathite, heard about all the troubles that had come upon him, they set out from their homes and met together by agreement to go and sympathize with him and comfort him. When they saw him from a distance, they could hardly recognize him; they began to weep aloud, and they tore their robes and sprinkled dust on their heads. Then they sat on the ground with him for seven days and seven nights. No one said a word to him, because they saw how great his suffering was. (Job 2:11-13)

This was exactly the right way to connect with Job. They didn't come with quick advice to make him feel better, and they didn't leave too soon. From looking at their actions, we can see three things they did well:

(1) *THEY SHOWED UP FOR THEIR FRIEND.*
They didn't wait for him to call and invite them to come; they just came. When a person is in trouble, our presence means more than anything else. I've known some people (and you know them, too) who

aren't content with just showing up—they insist on taking control and giving unsolicited advice. Sometimes, people really appreciate that approach, but this behavior more often annoys those who are grieving and adds to their pain. Figure out the difference.

(2) THEY WEPT WITH JOB.

They felt at least a little of what Job was feeling. A friend doesn't laugh when we're sad, and he doesn't find fault when we're thrilled that God has done something wonderful. Emotional empathy is a sure sign of a true friendship. Some people are more guarded in their emotions. They may see themselves as the alpha personality who takes charge of every situation. There's nothing wrong with being a leader, but in that moment of grief, people need us to follow the admonition to "weep with those who weep and rejoice with those who rejoice" (Romans 12:15).

(3) THEY SPENT PLENTY OF TIME RELATING TO JOB'S PAIN BEFORE THEY SAID A WORD.

I was at a funeral of a man who had died in car accident, leaving his wife to raise their three small children. At the funeral, a lady rushed up to her, hugged her, and said, "Tomorrow you'll feel a lot better. God is on the throne. It'll be all right." I wanted to grab her arm and escort her out, but that would have added to the awkwardness of the moment. When people are in pain, our words aren't the answer, at least as they first come to grips with their loss. Our presence and our tears are the only proper response.

✗ WHAT THEY DID WRONG

When the three friends opened their mouths, they blew it. When they began to speak, Job should have said, "Hey, not so fast!" Again and again, they blamed Job for his troubles. They drew a straight line from cause to effect, or actually, from effect back to cause. They made several errors that added to Job's heartache:

① *THEY DIDN'T SPEAK THE TRUTH.*

They were sure that the only possible explanation for the series of catastrophes was that Job had sinned and God was punishing him. And they were dead wrong. They were wrong about the cause of Job's problems, and they were wrong about God's purposes. Their accusations and Job's defense go on for about twenty-six chapters. Near the end of the book, God shows up, but instead of answering Job's specific questions, He challenges Job's limited perspective and assures him that He is more powerful, wiser, and more creative than Job can imagine. Then, God indicts the three friends for their hard hearts and false assumptions:

> "I am angry with you and your two friends, because you have not spoken the truth about me, as my servant Job has. So now take seven bulls and seven rams and go to my servant Job and sacrifice a burnt offering for yourselves. My servant Job will pray for you, and I will accept his prayer and not deal with you according to your folly. You have not spoken the truth about me, as my servant Job has." So Eliphaz the Temanite, Bildad the Shuhite and Zophar the Naamathite did what the LORD told them; and the LORD accepted Job's prayer. (Job 42:7-9)

② *THEY BLAMED JOB INSTEAD OF COMFORTING HIM.*

So much for the first seven days! The friends took the easy way out. They didn't want to wrestle with the complexities of life, the many different causes of suffering, and the mysterious purposes of God. To them (and to many Christians today) the simple answer is the preferred answer: "It's your fault, so stop it!" I've heard people bring up "Achan in the camp" when someone was grieving a tragic loss. I wished I could go back and intervene before those toxic words were spoken, but I couldn't. The damage had been done.

(3) THEY PERSONALIZED THEIR BLAME.

When Amy tells me that something I said or did hurt her, I can hear it. I don't want to hear it, but I value our relationship too much to discount it. However, Amy doesn't reach the conclusion that, "because you did that, you're a terrible person!" But that's exactly what Job's friends did. They were wrong to blame him for his troubles, and they were even more wrong to conclude that he was a terrible person because he refused to accept their accusation. Satan is called "the accuser of the brethren," and when we condemn a person's identity, we're on Satan's team, voicing his message, having the impact he wants to have on the person who is listening. To put it another way, when someone points out a behavior in us that's self-destructive, we can usually accept their input, but when they use our vulnerability to shame us, they've become like Job's friends.

PAINT A PICTURE

The processing stage isn't about blaming, punishing, dominating, controlling, or fixing the person's problems. It's about restoration. Recall that in Paul's letter to the Galatians, he encouraged us to pursue that end: "You who live by the Spirit should restore that person gently. But watch yourselves, or you also may be tempted. Carry each other's burdens, and in this way you will fulfill the law of Christ" (Galatians 6:1-2). He warned, "watch yourselves" because we might be tempted. Tempted to do what? To blame, punish, dominate, control, or try to make ourselves into "indispensable heroes" by coming to the rescue to fix another person's problems. Are these real temptations? You bet they are! We need to be careful we don't use another person's trust to go on a power trip. Our demeanor should be one of compassionate curiosity, not arrogant pride from believing we're the person's only hope of help and progress. I try to ask questions much more frequently than offering answers.

We see a terrific example of helping someone process a personal flaw in the conversation between King David and the prophet Nathan. Before their talk, David had committed multiple sins and crimes. He had committed adultery with his friend Uriah's wife, Bathsheba, and when she got pregnant, he tried to cover his sin by bringing Uriah home from the battlelines (where David should have been) to have sex with his wife. When this didn't work, David sent a message to his general to orchestrate an attack so that Uriah would be killed. It happened, but several other soldiers were also killed, so multiple men died to cover up David's sin.

David thought he had gotten away with it all, but Nathan knew better, and he was incredibly skilled in the art of speaking the truth. The Lord sent Nathan to David, where the prophet told the king a story that was sure to touch his heart:

> "There were two men in a certain town, one rich and the other poor. The rich man had a very large number of sheep and cattle, but the poor man had nothing except one little ewe lamb he had bought. He raised it, and it grew up with him and his children. It shared his food, drank from his cup and even slept in his arms. It was like a daughter to him.
>
> Now a traveler came to the rich man, but the rich man refrained from taking one of his own sheep or cattle to prepare a meal for the traveler who had come to him.

Instead, he took the ewe lamb that belonged to the poor man and prepared it for the one who had come to him." (2 Samuel 12:1-4)

David reacted just as Nathan anticipated. He was furious at the selfish man and snarled, "As surely as the LORD lives, the man who did this must die! He must pay for that lamb four times over, because he did such a thing and had no pity."

That was Nathan's opening. He looked at David and said, "You are the man!" Then he closed the loop so David couldn't deny, rationalize, minimize, or excuse his behavior:

> "This is what the LORD, the God of Israel, says: 'I anointed you king over Israel, and I delivered you from the hand of Saul. I gave your master's house to you, and your master's wives into your arms. I gave you all Israel and Judah. And if all this had been too little, I would have given you even more. Why did you despise the word of the LORD by doing what is evil in his eyes? You struck down Uriah the Hittite with the sword and took his wife to be your own. You killed him with the sword of the Ammonites. Now, therefore, the sword will never depart from your house, because you despised me and took the wife of Uriah the Hittite to be your own.'" (vv. 7-10)

David responded, "I have sinned against the Lord" (v. 13). Nathan assured David of God's forgiveness, but he was also honest about the consequences of his choices.

Do you think Nathan spent time thinking and praying about what he was going to say to David? Of course! God gave him a way—a story—to get underneath David's skin. David's exaggerated reaction is very common when someone describes another person's sin that's like our own. Those who lie violently condemn someone who lies to them; those who steal or embezzle have no patience for those who sin in the same way; those who gossip can't stand it when others gossip about them. David's reaction let Nathan know that David identified with the selfish man in the story.

Years ago, a pastor asked me to come to his church to meet with him and speak on Sunday morning. I'd heard glowing stories about him. He was a powerful leader, a gifted speaker, and a compassionate pastor. His people loved him . . . but they didn't love his wife. She was exacting, demeaning, and demanding. She didn't mind people overhearing her when she berated her husband in the lobby of the church, in the halls of the church office, or at restaurants around town. I met with a number of people in the church during those days, and they all had the same observation: she was a pain, and he was a saint for putting up with her. Both characterizations were inaccurate and concerning to me.

I asked him if I could tell him a story. I wasn't as creative as the prophet Nathan, but I thought it fit really well. I told him about a man who was a popular public speaker. He wore an Army uniform, and his messages were about patriotism and courage under fire. He amazed audiences with firsthand accounts of his heroics in battle . . . until someone looked up his record and discovered he was a fraud. He had never been in combat, and in fact, he had never served in any branch of the military. His lie is a criminal offense commonly called "stolen valor." I told the pastor who was listening, "It's interesting that the man used a uniform to show on the outside what he wasn't on the inside. I've been with you for several days, and I've watched people in your church treat you like you're a victim. That's the uniform you're wearing to convince people of something that isn't really true." He looked surprised at my honesty. I continued, "Brother, I don't buy it. I'm calling 'stolen valor' on you. You're not a victim. You're powerful, you're gifted, and the Spirit of God is on you. Your wife deserves better than living with someone pretending to be a victim."

At that moment, he broke down and asked, "Would you go to my home with me? I want to talk with my wife about this."

To be honest, I wished my flight home was leaving in ten minutes, but I said, "Sure." We went to his house, and I mostly watched and listened as he told his wife, "We've been living this way much too long. I've been wrong in playing the role of a victim, and I've had payoffs of people feeling sorry for me and thinking I'm noble for putting up with your bad moods. And I ask for your forgiveness."

She looked stunned and started to defend herself, but he continued, "But honey, you've been wrong in using your negativity to control me, and I want you to know, that's stopping right now. It isn't good for me, and it isn't good for you. From this point on, I'm going to live in truth. I hope you'll join me, but even if you don't, I'm not going back to being a victim ever again." A few months later, he called me to report that their marriage was stronger than it had ever been. I wish I could say all my process conversations went this well this quickly, but lives are often really messy and this stage usually takes much more time.

SELF-DISCOVERY

It's not our role to tell people how to think, feel, and act. Our job is to hold up a light so they can see themselves more clearly so they can make better decisions—about what to believe, what's true and not true, how to grieve, and how to experience love more fully. Self-discovery is far more powerful than giving advice. I sometimes make observations, but I almost never say, "Here's what you need to do."

I've learned that great questions are incredibly valuable. I've landed on several I use when I'm helping someone in the processing stage. After the person has disclosed events, as well as perceptions and emotions about those events, I often ask:

* HOW DID THIS BEGIN?

* WHAT'S YOUR EARLIEST MEMORY OF THIS?

* WHAT'S THE WIN FOR THIS FALSE BELIEF OR SELF-DESTRUCTIVE BEHAVIOR?

* HOW'S IT WORKING FOR YOU? ARE YOU REALLY WINNING?

* WHAT COULD THIS COST YOU IF NOTHING CHANGES?

* IS IT WORTH IT TO GET A BETTER HANDLE ON IT?

* DO YOU REALLY WANT TO BE FREE FROM THIS?

* WHAT DO YOU THINK YOU CAN DO ABOUT IT?

* WHAT DO YOU WANT TO DO ABOUT IT?

* WHEN DO YOU WANT TO START MAKING CHANGES?
    (SETTING A DATE IMPLIES SERIOUSNESS.)

Many of us are very uncomfortable with tears. When someone cries, we rush in to provide comfort—supposedly for their sake, but my guess is that it's too often because their tears make us feel awkward. If you want to be a friend at this stage, you need to become more comfortable when the person has a tear in his or her eye. Your presence and your patience are plenty of comfort. Tears are a sign the Lord has opened a door that has been shut for a long time, and the long-buried emotions are finally being expressed. If we do something to stop them, we short-circuit what God wants to do in that person's life.

How long should we let someone cry? As long as it takes. A lady from a verbally and emotionally abusive home cried for days when friend asked some pointed questions and let her express whatever came up from the abyss of her heart. It was, she now says, the turning point in her life, her marriage, her relationship with her three children, and her career. Her prolonged weeping was awkward . . . but necessary.

We can tell people what to do, but it's much more effective when they discover their own path forward. If we tell them what to do and how to feel, it's *our* process, and it's up to us to make change happen. That's not good for anybody! These questions, and any others you find helpful, encourage self-discovery and ownership by the person we're helping. And if you're the person processing your pain, don't expect your friend or mentor to tell you every step to take. At the beginning of this stage, you may feel overwhelmed, but sooner or later, grieving will bring real healing. Then you can be an adult, be strong, and take your life in your hands.

I love the story of Jesus and Zacchaeus, not because I can sing about him being a little guy who climbed up a sycamore tree, but for the end of the story. For some context, Luke tells us that Zacchaeus was a "chief tax collector." That's not the role of a career IRS employee who lives down the street. It's much more like a Mafia don who extorts money in a protection racket. (Now, are you thinking about him a little differently?) After Jesus invited himself to dinner, the door closes and we hear nothing of their conversation. Then, when they come out again, Zacchaeus stands up and proclaims, "Look, Lord! Here and now I give half of my possessions to the

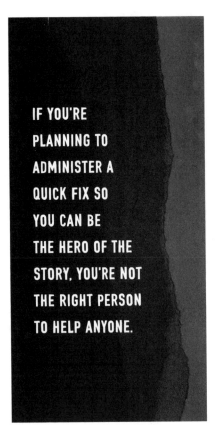

IF YOU'RE PLANNING TO ADMINISTER A QUICK FIX SO YOU CAN BE THE HERO OF THE STORY, YOU'RE NOT THE RIGHT PERSON TO HELP ANYONE.

poor, and if I have cheated anybody out of anything, I will pay back four times the amount" (Luke 19:8). Whatever happened in the context of their meal together transformed the little man's heart. Jesus didn't give him a spreadsheet with ways he had cheated people and amounts he needed to pay back. Grace made the difference, and Zacchaeus owned his sin and his repentance.

Jesus affirmed his decision: "Today salvation has come to this house, because this man, too, is a son of Abraham. For the Son of Man came to seek and to save the lost" (vv. 9-10). Don't you know Jesus was beaming when He looked at Zacchaeus and spoke those words?

That's part of our role, too. When the pastor found the courage to speak the truth about "wearing his uniform" of being a victim and spoke to his wife about necessary changes he was making, I thought of Jesus celebrating that day at Zacchaeus's house. And when the pastor called me to give me the great report of real progress in his marriage, I celebrated with him again.

Let's be realistic. The problems that surface when people disclose their secrets and begin to process them have been with them for years, maybe decades, and they aren't resolved in a conversation or two. In most cases, this is by far the messiest stage because the hardest things in their lives are finally brought out into the light. The reason people live so long in denial is that the truth is so threatening, so don't expect quick progress to heal deep wounds and resolve huge problems.

If you're planning to administer a quick fix so you can be the hero of the story, you're not the right person to help anyone at this stage. Take a hard look at your own motives and stay in the process for your own sake first. But after you've made sufficient progress yourself, you can be an incredible friend to those who need help. We've looked at a number of passages from Proverbs in this chapter. Let me point to one more: "A friend loves at all times, and a brother [or sister] is born for a time of adversity" (Proverbs 17:17). In *The Merchant of Venice*, Shakespeare echoes Solomon's observation:

> The quality of mercy is not strained.
> It droppeth as the gentle rain from heaven
> Upon the place beneath. It is twice blest;
> It blesseth him that gives and him that takes . . . [34]

That means that our care isn't forced or stretched thin by our need to look like saviors. It means we're not impatient to fix the person and move on. We come alive when we're involved in people's lives at this level. It's the most challenging and rewarding role we can play, but as I've said now many times, "Do Not Pass Go" if you're not yet ready to help people in this way.

REZ.CHURCH

10 Year Anniversary Party

AMY & ME WITH
SKYLAR, KIM-WALKER SMITH,
SIMEON MYERS & JOEL BODKER

June 19, 2020

1

Write your definition or description of a "wounded healer."

....

....

....

....

....

....

....

....

2

What are some payoffs of "perception management"? What are the costs?

....

....

....

....

....

....

....

....

3

Have you ever received prolonged, unhurried, tender care when you were grieving? What did that mean to you?

....
....
....
....
....
....
....
....
....
....

4

Has anyone ever treated you like Job's friends treated him when they opened their mouths? If so, how did their accusations (or other forms of insensitivity) affect you?

....
....
....
....
....
....
....
....
....
....

5

How does (or would)
having a readily available
set of questions give you
confidence as you help
someone process pain?

....

....

....

....

....

....

....

....

....

....

6

Are you ready to help
others in this stage? Why
or why not? Who would
say you are? Who would
say you're not? How do
you weigh their input?

....

....

....

....

....

....

....

....

....

Five Stages of Connection

STAGE 1

RELATE

WE WALK TOGETHER.

STAGE 2

TRUST

WE SHARE OUR STORIES.

STAGE 3

DISCLOSE

WE CONFESS OUR FAULTS
TO EACH OTHER.

STAGE 4

PROCESS

WE SUBMIT TO EACH OTHER.

STAGE 5

INTEGRATE

WE ACCEPT GOD'S GRACE.

CHAPTER ELEVEN

INTEGRATE

So far in our process, it's as if we've been walking into a dark basement, turning on the light, and opening the doors to all the closets to let the trapped critters out. Sometimes we realize they're more vicious and dangerous than we hoped, but more often, we discover their roar has been amplified in the confined space of the basement. For a long time, our fears have kept the truth in the dark, but no longer.

Whenever I've followed the process outlined in this book, God has given me a different perspective on the Great Commandment. As we've seen, an expert in Jewish law asked Jesus, "Teacher, what must I do to inherit eternal life." He answered, "Love the Lord your God with all your heart and with all your soul and with all your strength and with all your mind" (Luke 10:27).

For a long time, I wasn't willing or able to love God with all my heart because so many of my perceptions about God, about myself, and about others were clouded with shame. But as the light was turned on in the basement, I've been able to bring all of my heart to God in prayer and let deeper experiences of His love replace my shame with security.

In the past, I wasn't willing or able to love God with *all* my soul because my emotions were too threatening to me, so I repressed them. But when the light was turned on, I've experienced God's healing touch as I've grieved the losses I've endured.

I wasn't willing or able to love God with *all* my strength because I vacillated between not believing I had any strength or trusting in my strength more than God's. But as I've begun to walk in the light, I can accept my strengths as gifts from God and use them humbly and joyfully.

And I wasn't willing or able to love God with *all* my mind because I was believing so many lies about myself and Him. But as the lights came on, I've been able to identify the false beliefs and correct them with God's truth.

Jesus' response to the Jewish law expert was insightful and challenging, but He wasn't quite finished. He concluded, "And . . . 'love your neighbor as yourself'" (v. 27). I can't tell you how many Christians I've talked to who despise themselves. They call themselves horrible names and continually berate their abilities, their motives, and their desires. Their shame has found an outlet in self-hatred. As Jesus connected the internal and the external, He said, "Out of the abundance of the heart [the] mouth speaks" (Luke 6:45 NKJV). We can't fulfill God's greatest commandment to love Him and love others until and unless we experience His love for us. I realized I couldn't love people if my heart wasn't overflowing with God's love for me.

You might want to say, "But Jonathan, didn't you already know all that?" Yes, I knew it, but I didn't *really* know it. I'm sure you know what I mean. I could teach and preach for hours about the love of God, but until God took the locks off the doors in the basement of my heart, I couldn't experience

God's tenderness, kindness, and affirmation. Poet and playwright T. S. Eliot wrote, "We shall not cease from exploration, and the end of all our exploring will be to arrive where we started and know the place for the first time." [35] That has been my experience.

In the past, you might have seen "a work Jonathan," "a friend Jonathan," and "a family Jonathan," but those personas were often very different. As I've found safe people with whom I can confidently relate, trust, disclose, and process, I no longer need to play different roles in different parts of my life. No more compartmentalizing. No more masks. No more hiding. No more posing. When we learn to integrate what we've learned into every aspect of our lives, we can accept our strengths without pride because we realize they're gifts from God, and we can accept our flaws without shame because they keep us looking to God for forgiveness and transformation.

Think of a home as a metaphor for the stages:

- When we *relate*, we're talking to neighbors who have come into our yard for some burgers we're grilling.

- When we *trust*, we're inviting them into the house where they see the pictures on the wall as we tell them about our family.

- When we *disclose*, we let people know we have closets in the basement, but we don't let them go down there.

- When we *process*, we take them into the basement, turn on the light, and open the doors to reveal what's been there so long.

- And when we *integrate*, a reliable friend helps us run off the critters, clean out the closets, and keep the doors open.

Integration is the state of wholeness that results from the intentional removal of the defense mechanisms that fragment our lives, our identities, and our relationships. To hide our deficiencies and protect our hearts, we use all kinds of ways to keep people from knowing the truth about us. To be sure, some of us have been in relationships that are so toxic and abusive that we were forced to protect ourselves from more harm. In these situations, self-protection is necessary, not pathological. But most of us have used those strategies with people who aren't threats, and even with people who are safe and loving. It's time to intentionally remove them.

AGENTS OF GRACE

I'm afraid many Christians have a very limited concept of God's grace. It's much more than a ticket to heaven; it's the power of God to transform us, strengthen us, and guide us so that we live full, confident, God-honoring lives. When we experience grace, we not only admit our weaknesses—we truly believe that God uses our weaknesses for good in us . . . and then through us, in others.

We can't dispense grace to others, though, if we haven't experienced it. Or to put it more accurately, we only have the ability and resources to impart grace to others to the extent that we've experienced God's love, forgiveness, and acceptance in the depths of our own hearts—to that extent, and no more.

Jesus said, "Truly I tell you, whatever you bind on earth will be bound in heaven, and whatever you loose on earth will be loosed in heaven" (Matthew 18:18). This verse has many implications, and one of them is that when we release grace in our relationships, God releases grace from heaven into the lives of those people. In partnership with the Holy Spirit, we're agents of grace. We loosen people from their shame, their depression, their bitterness, their addiction, and any other problems that have persistently afflicted them. Condemnation doesn't release them; it only reinforces the problem and locks the closet doors. But loving them enough to speak the truth—the truth about their problem, but also the truth about God's amazing love—gives them the courage to walk in the light of that truth.

We aren't on our own. Before Jesus was arrested, He told His disciples that He was sending "another Counselor" (sometimes translated "Comforter"), the Holy Spirit. Both those words can be misunderstood—He's not a camp counselor, and He's not a quilt. The word there is better translated "Advocate," a defense attorney, and we have two on our defense team: the Spirit and Jesus. When the accuser alleges that our sin is unforgivable, that we're beyond the love of God, and that we're worthless, the Spirit is our advocate. He whispers to us that we're God's delight, His beloved children, and the apple of His eye.

Jesus plays a similar role on the defense team. In his first letter, John explained, "My little children, these things I write to you, so that you may

> **INTEGRATION IS THE STAGE OF THE WHOLENESS THAT RESULTS FROM THE INTENTIONAL REMOVAL OF THE DEFENSE MECHANISMS THAT FRAGMENT OUR LIVES, OUR IDENTITIES, & OUR RELATIONSHIPS.**

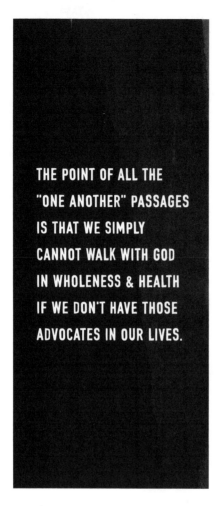

THE POINT OF ALL THE "ONE ANOTHER" PASSAGES IS THAT WE SIMPLY CANNOT WALK WITH GOD IN WHOLENESS & HEALTH IF WE DON'T HAVE THOSE ADVOCATES IN OUR LIVES.

not sin. And if anyone sins, we have an Advocate with the Father, Jesus Christ the righteous. And He Himself is the propitiation for our sins, and not for ours only but also for the whole world" (1 John 2:1-2 NKJV).

Jesus didn't just sit at the table to argue our case. He stepped in front of the judge and said, "I'll pay what Jonathan owes." And He paid what you owe. He takes our sins, our brokenness, and our defectiveness, and He gives us His forgiveness, His righteousness, and His heart. When we sin, we don't have to defend ourselves any longer because Jesus has already paid the price. We can be completely honest with God, with no shame and no hiding, because we know we're already forgiven and we're totally known and loved. *Propitiation* means "to satisfy the wrath that is deserved." Jesus did that for us. Yes, sin is a big problem, but Jesus' love is far greater. He took our sin, and He gave us His righteousness.

That's the incredible swap Paul described in his second letter to the Corinthians: "God made [Jesus] who had no sin to be sin for us, so that in him we might become the righteousness of God" (2 Corinthians 5:21). Over and over again, especially in Paul's letters, we're described as being "in

Christ" or "in Him." We're in Christ in His death, so His payment for sin is applied to us. We're in Christ in His life, so His righteousness is credited to us. We're in Christ in His resurrection, so His supernatural life is infused into us. And we're in Christ in His ascension to the throne at the right hand of the Father, so we're given authority to reign with Him.

In the courtroom, the sentence has been paid, and we've been set free to honor the one who loves us so much. The Holy Spirit and Jesus smile and ask us, "Where are your accusers?" They've been eternally silenced.

In our spiritual friendships, we're advocates of one another. No, we don't pay for each other's sins, but we're junior partners in the law firm, and we step into each other's lives to speak truth, comfort, and affirmation. The point of all the "one another" passages is that we simply cannot walk with God in wholeness and health if we don't have those advocates in our lives. It's not a flaw that we need each other. That's the way God designed His body to function, and it only functions well when we're healthy and whole.

Every time I feel "less than" and every time I feel attacked by my own poisonous thoughts, my friends step in to challenge my perceptions. In a lot of ways, they ask the same question, "Jonathan, where are your accusers?" In other words, "We're standing with you in the courtroom, and the case has already been decided. You're free! Your debt has been paid! And even better, the judge and the two lead defenders love you to death!"

CATCH AND RELEASE

We all have accusers, and some are more aggressive than others. None, however, are too threatening for our heavenly advocates to handle. John describes a scene from the life of Jesus that was basically R-rated. Let's take a look:

> At dawn [Jesus] appeared again in the temple courts, where all the people gathered around him, and he sat down to teach them. The teachers of the law and the Pharisees brought in a woman caught in adultery. They made her stand before the group and said to Jesus, "Teacher, this woman was caught in the act of adultery. In the Law Moses commanded us to stone such women. Now what do you say?" They were using this question as a trap, in order to have a basis for accusing him.
>
> But Jesus bent down and started to write on the ground with his finger. When they kept on questioning him, he straightened up and said to them, "Let any one of you who is without sin be the first to throw a stone at her." Again he stooped down and wrote on the ground.
>
> At this, those who heard began to go away one at a time, the older ones first, until only Jesus was left, with the woman still standing there. Jesus straightened up and asked her, "Woman, where are they? Has no one condemned you?"
>
> "No one, sir," she said.
>
> "Then neither do I condemn you," Jesus declared. "Go now and leave your life of sin." (John 8:2-11)

And you think you've been embarrassed! Imagine this scene. The temple was still under construction when Jesus was there. It was an imposing structure, with high stone walls, beautiful gates, and a bustling crowd. As Jesus was teaching, some religious leaders dragged a woman they'd caught having sex with a man who wasn't her husband. (We might wonder why they didn't bring the man along, but that's a different topic for discussion.)

Did they let her grab her clothes on the way out? What was the look on her face? What was the tone of voice of her accusers? They claimed they wanted justice, but they really wanted to shame her and test Jesus to see if all of His talk about love and forgiveness extended to someone like her. (Surely not her!) Jesus didn't take the bait. Instead, He obliterated their attacks on her and Him. They wanted Him to join them in condemning her, but instead, He became her advocate.

Let me draw some principles from this account about having Jesus as your defense.

YOU WON'T BE INTIMIDATED OR CONTROLLED BY COERCIVE INFLUENCES OR TACTICS.

The woman faced humiliating exposure, condemnation, and death. She was defenseless when they grabbed her and dragged her to the temple, but Jesus changed the trajectory of the story. I'm sure the religious leaders had passages from their Scriptures to back them up, but they missed the heart of God. For this woman and for us, we need to be very wary of religious zealots who have no friends but are armed with a lot of Bible passages and hard hearts. They aren't "accurately handling the word of truth."

Who would you rather have sitting on the bench in the courtroom: people who want to destroy you, or someone who has proven His love by going to the extreme of dying in your place, someone who loves you as much as the Father loves Him? Jesus' love doesn't turn a blind eye to sin. He acknowledges it, but He assures us that He has paid the price for it. Paul says that Jesus intercedes for us. He's praying for you and me right now!

(2) YOU'LL USE THE SCRIPTURE TO BUILD PEOPLE UP AND TEAR DOWN SPIRITUAL STRONGHOLDS—NOT TO TEAR PEOPLE DOWN AND CREATE STRONGHOLDS.

Some people study the Bible so they can win arguments, but that's not why God gave His Word to us. Many medications have inscriptions on the bottle: "Use only as prescribed." That's what we need to write on the spine of our Bibles. At the temple that day, the religious leaders were misusing the words of God to condemn the woman and trap Jesus, and they believed they were completely righteous in using the Scriptures that way.

(3) YOU'LL TAKE WHAT IS AT FACE VALUE AND YOU WON'T BE HAUNTED OR BROWBEATEN BY WHAT "SHOULD BE."

Jesus didn't react in fear or anger. He was completely self-assured. In fact, He didn't even answer the woman's accusers directly at all. If He had asked the woman what was going on, she probably would have said, "I should have known better!" I've talked to countless people who live in Shouldsville, and they can't find the road out. When I've asked innocuous questions like, "How's your marriage?" or "How are your kids?" they respond, "You know, Pastor, I should be a better spouse, and I know I should be there more for my kids. I'm trying. I'll do better." I feel like I need to jump in and say, "Hey, it's just a question. I'm not accusing you. You're not in trouble. I'm not asking what you should be. I'm only asking about what's actually going on right now. No judgment. No condemnation."

That's what I think was going on when Jesus wrote in the dust. He may have been writing verses about their sins, showing how hypocritical they were to accuse the woman. They had come to kill, but Jesus was there to forgive and restore. I believe He was more than willing to forgive and restore them, too, but the best they could do was walk away. They had come to shame the woman, but they went away with a new realization of their own sinfulness.

In the stage of integration, we focus on what is, not what should be. We learn to live in the present, not the haunted past or with daydreams of a magical future.

④ YOU'LL SURROUND YOURSELF WITH COMMUNITY, BUT NOT ACCUSERS.

For years, I envisioned the end of this scene as Jesus and the woman sitting alone, but that's not what the passage says. The accusers couldn't take the bright light of Jesus, so they left, but the crowds of people who were watching stuck around. We need to surround ourselves with people who take pleasure in our redemption, and we need to avoid others who take pleasure in our faults. Are we sponges who soak up the venom other people spew? Or do we have confidence that God's love and strength enables us to resist every temptation to join the accuser and blast ourselves?

⑤ YOU WON'T FEAR PERSONAL FREEDOM. INSTEAD YOU'LL VIEW FREEDOM AS THE SHORTEST ROUTE TO RESPONSIBILITY & GROWTH.

I know Christians who are terrified of the freedom God has given them in Christ. They either don't trust God to guide them or they don't trust themselves to make good decisions. They become rule-keepers, shackled to a set of do's and don'ts. Instead of enjoying their freedom, they act like they're in jail serving their sentence, or at best, on probation under the scowling eye of their probation officer. Jesus didn't tell the woman, "Okay, I ran them off, but I'm putting an ankle bracelet on you to monitor your movements so you don't go near your boyfriend again." Jesus removed the accusers, demonstrated grace, gave her one instruction, and then let her enjoy her new freedom.

As we've seen, if our spirituality is based on law and rules, we'll be arrogant when we're obeying and ashamed when we're not. But faith based on God's grace draws us close to Him and motivates us to use our freedom to honor Him and bless others. Many Christians are sure God judges them based on their performance, and they can't really imagine living any other way. In the stage of integration, grace finds its way into the closet to expose the lie and free the captive . . . and maybe that's you.

As we experience the freedom that comes from being forgiven and loved by God, we'll offer other people the same blessing. We won't have a checklist for our spouse, our kids, our coworkers, and our friends to follow before we consider them acceptable. (For our kids, we gradually decrease the rules as they mature and become fully functioning, wise, responsible adults.)

BETTER CONCLUSIONS

When I talked to the people on our team about the stage of integration, we had a wonderful conversation. They made some observations that capture what this part of the journey is all about:

- To reject the integrated life is to reject God's grace.

- When I'm my own defender:
  — *I have to keep score to know if I'm doing better than someone else.*

— I carry the debt of my own sins.

— I point out the debt of others' sins.

— I make people follow my rules so they'll be more acceptable.

↑ ALL OF THESE ARE A POOR SUBSTITUTE FOR GENUINE ↑
DEVOTION TO CHRIST AND A LIFE THAT HONORS HIM.

- An integrated life is genuine holiness. The pursuit of this life draws you closer to God and people. It calls you out of hiding to be found and known . . . out of darkness and into the light of God's grace.

- An integrated life is the essence of God's design for us and the fulfillment of His purposes described throughout the Bible. In Matthew's account of Jesus talking about the Great Commandment, he reports Jesus saying that loving God and people sums up the entire message of the Bible: "All the Law and the Prophets hang on these two commandments" (Matthew 22:37-40).

If Jesus hadn't been there when the religious leaders brought the woman to the temple, she might have been violently exposed, permanently labeled, mercilessly judged, and ultimately destroyed. But instead, Jesus valued her, so He defended her, rescued her, and released her with an opportunity to write a new ending to her story.

Do you know Jesus as your advocate against your accusers? Whether condemning voices speak in your mind or come from the lips of hateful people, Jesus is there to defend you. If the accusations are untrue, Jesus will affirm you. If they're true, remember that Jesus paid the price for you and set you free. Our advocate is holy, righteous, and good. The psalmist wrote, "For the LORD is our defense; and the Holy One of Israel is our king" (Psalm 89:18 KJV).

Do you have people in your life who are junior partners on the defense team? They aren't optional equipment. These people are absolutely necessary for you to become the man or woman God wants you to be.

And are you this kind of friend for someone else? Are you on the defense team taking the case to advocate for someone you know? Jesus told His disciples (and us), "Follow Me." When we follow Him, we'll step into the mess of other people's lives to notice them, defend them, care for them, and release them into a new sense of freedom and joy.

consider
THIS

1

In the metaphor of people coming to your house, who have you allowed the most freedom to walk around and notice things? How far have you allowed that person to come in? What (if anything) is preventing you from opening the closet doors in the basement and turning on the lights?

....

....

....

....

....

2

What does it mean to be a "junior partner" on a defense team with the Holy Spirit and Jesus as the primary advocates? Are you playing that role in anyone's life? Explain your answer.

....

....

....

....

....

....

3

In John's account of
Jesus, the religious
leaders, and the woman
caught in adultery, put
yourself in the woman's
place. At each moment,
from her apprehension,
to the temple in front
of Jesus and the
crowd, and then after
the accusers left, how
would you have felt?

....

....

....

....

....

....

....

....

....

4

Describe the power
that "shoulds"
have in the lives of
people you know.
And describe the power
they have in your life.

....

....

....

....

....

....

....

....

....

....

5

Now that you've read
the chapter, how
would you describe
"an integrated life"?

....

....

....

....

....

....

....

....

....

....

....

....

....

....

....

....

....

....

....

....

....

IF CHRIST LIVES IN US
CONTROLLING OUR PERSONALITIES,
WE WILL LEAVE
GLORIOUS MARKS
ON THE LIVES WE TOUCH.
NOT BECAUSE OF OUR
LOVELY CHARACTERS BUT
BECAUSE OF HIS.

— Eugenia Price —

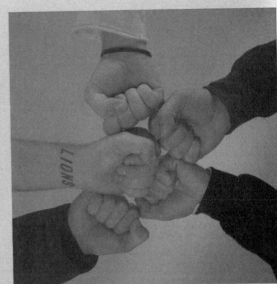

THE LIONS
DECEMBER 2020

JEREMY + SETHRY + ZACH C. + ISAIAH + JAMES + ANDREW + ME + JOSHUA + LANDON + TY + ZACH S.

INTRODUCING NEWBORN SARAH TO
BIG SISTER MADELYN & BIG BROTHER NATHAN
AUGUST 2002

CHAPTER TWELVE

COLLATERAL REDEMPTION

At a Saturday evening church service several years ago, my message was about forgiveness. Near the end, I enthusiastically proclaimed, "There's no such thing as an unforgivable person!" When the service was over, a man waited to talk to me. I'd never seen him before, so I assumed it was his first time to visit Rez. After I spoke to a number of others and I was finally alone, he walked up, shook my hand and said, "I'm Sean Wheeler. I'd like to ask you a question."

I was all set to give him a profound biblical nugget that would transform his life. I said, "Sure, fire away."

He asked the most frightening question anyone can ask a pastor: "Do you really believe what you preached?"

I quickly did a mental scan of all the points in my sermon, checking for anything I might have inflated or exaggerated. "Yeah," I told him, "I believe every word."

I was all set for an extended post-church, pre-dinner debate, but instead, tears welled in his eyes, and he asked, "Well, what if I don't know their names? And what if I've never seen their faces?"

I said softly, "Sean, talk to me. Tell me what's going on. I don't really understand."

He explained that for two years when he was a little boy, he had been trafficked. He had been blindfolded, molested, and filmed. He had been too young to fight back. Each time, he was completely helpless.

Now I understood. I let it sink in for a few seconds, and I told him, "Sean, it's okay. God knows their names."

For the next few weeks, I noticed Sean every weekend at church. He sat in the very back, paying close attention to everything. Eventually, he moved a little closer to the front, then a few seats closer. After a few months, he was sitting on the front row, singing and dancing his praise to God with all his heart. It was one of the most beautiful things I've ever seen in my life!

I knew that Mike, one of the people on our team, was meeting with Sean, so I asked him, "What in the world has happened to Sean? It looks like God has done something fantastic!"

Mike told me that a few weeks before, our receptionist received a phone call from a lonely and broken man in our community. He explained that he was arrested for possession of child pornography, and he felt very alone. The court imposes restrictions on those offenders so they can't go to grocery stores or anywhere else children are present during the days and evenings. He said, "I've heard your church loves people. Is there anyone who would be willing to come where I'm staying and visit with me? I just want someone to talk to."

The request went to the men's ministry. Mike told the group about the man's request and asked, "Is anyone here willing to visit him?" Sean raised his hand. He made the call, set up a time to visit, and went to his house. There, Sean listened to the man's story, and then he told him his story. For weeks, Sean kept going to see him. Sean was able to tell the man about the damage he had suffered, but he explained, "But that's not the end of my story, and your story doesn't have to end here either." He told the man about Jesus and the difference forgiveness has made in his life.

Today, Sean is one of the most life-giving people I know. He's the only person I've ever heard about who has been a victim of child sex trafficking and now goes to prisons to share the love of Jesus with the perpetrators. Sean let the love and light of God into the deepest recesses of his broken heart, and God has done an amazing work in him. He will tell you that he still has a long way to go to mend the damaged parts, but from what I can see, he's well on his way. He's no longer hiding, no longer shackled by shame, and no longer sees himself as a victim. He has something powerful to say to a group of people who desperately need to experience God's forgiveness and transforming power. Sean is on a mission. He's living an integrated life. We often talk about the ripples of collateral damage that spread to affect other people. Sean's ripple effect is *collateral redemption.*

HE REMEMBERED MY NAME

In the early 80s, Billy Hornsby, one of the founders of ARC, was a pastor in Monroe, Louisiana, about thirty miles from where our family lived. My dad knew him. In fact, in 1982, my dad sold Billy a red Chrysler with red interior (quite a car!). A few years later, my parents' marriage was very strained, and If anything, my dad's anger got worse. It was a hard time for all of us. I felt isolated and lonely. The only safe place was at my best friend's house, but my family situation caused my friend's family to withdraw from us. This left me feeling isolated from my friend. During this painful season, God brought a few people into my life: Miss Molly, Don Boyett (who is now my father-in-law), and Billy Hornsby.

I was only thirteen, but I remember very clearly the day that Billy came to our house to encourage my father, and then he spent some time with me. I guess he knew that I played the piano, so he sat down and played a few notes on the piano in our living room. After a few minutes, he turned to me and said, "Jonathan, this doesn't have to be the end. It can be a new beginning for you. Don't give up on God, and don't give up on the church." His kindness and attention meant the world to me.

Three years later after I left home, I started leading worship for Don Boyett at his church in Lake Providence, Louisiana. For $100 a week, I played the keyboard as I led the congregational singing. Pastors from all over the area got together once a year at a church pastored by Gary Ryals in southern Arkansas to hear speakers and rub shoulders with each other. Don often took me with him to these events. Billy was a popular speaker—actually, he was a legend—and he came fairly often. The first time I went, he was the speaker. I was sitting in the middle of the audience of about 200 pastors and staff members, but early in his message, he locked his eyes on me and nodded. After he spoke, I went up to him and started to introduce myself, but he didn't need me to say anything. He remembered my name. For my entire life, I'd felt isolated, ashamed, and defective, but the fact that Billy

Hornsby noticed me, nodded to me, and remembered my name spoke to my heart that I mattered to him. It was personal validation from someone everyone revered.

When Billy sat down with me in the living room and encouraged me not to give up, his words made a difference. And when he saw me at the pastors' events and remembered me, I felt valued. I sincerely doubt I'd be who I am and what I am today if he hadn't stopped to spend time with a thirteen year old kid whose family was imploding. It felt (and it was) a very unstable time. My brother and sister have great careers, and I suspect I would have found a good and challenging career, but I would have always carried the crushing burden of shame, I would have been afraid to let anyone know my secrets, and I would have remained an emotional exile even around wonderful people. I certainly wouldn't have the deep, honest, loving relationships I have with Amy and our children, and I wouldn't have any close friends because I'd have been too afraid to let anyone get too close. Billy's care for the "little guys" like me has resulted in multiplied collateral redemption in me and through me.

SKILLED AT RESTORATION

I think a lot of Christians, including Christian leaders, wear the trappings of spirituality but have missed the heart of God. I know people who read the Bible voraciously and spend time in prayer, but they're cruel . . . really cruel. I know people who stand up in front of an audience and talk about God's love, but their spouse and children are either terrified of them or desperate for their attention, unable to compete with the success of their careers. That's not the way of the cross and it's not the model of Jesus.

Wherever Jesus went, He touched people, restoring them physically, but also emotionally and spiritually. Even when He argued with the Pharisees, His goal was to convince them that their hearts were more important to God than rigid obedience to their ever-lengthening list of rules. The disciples watched Jesus again and again reach out to love, nurture, heal, and restore—and the Gospels give only a few snapshots from those incredibly packed three and a half years.

Paul was the smartest and toughest guy in the room, and then he met Jesus. The transformation didn't turn him from an assertive, driven man to a cupcake; instead, the Spirit changed his purpose and added a large dose of compassion. As we've seen, when he wrote his stern, corrective letter to the Galatians, he didn't just blast away and then wash his hands of them. His goal was to draw them back to the grace of God, and he encouraged them to "gently restore" those who had drifted from God and "carry each other's burdens, and in this way . . . fulfill the law of Christ" (Galatians 6:1-2). When people think of you and me, is that the image that comes to mind? Do they see us as supremely competent leaders of our churches, departments, businesses, and families? Do they see us enjoying the position of being high on a pedestal of respect? Or do they see us as leaders who are skilled at gently restoring those who are broken, sinful, and ashamed?

In another letter, Paul summed up the ethic of the Christian life by using the metaphor of changing clothes. He instructed the Colossians to "rid yourselves" of anger and slander, and to "put on the new self." Then he detailed what the "new self" will do: "Therefore, as God's chosen people, holy and dearly loved, clothe yourselves with compassion, kindness, humility, gentleness and patience. Bear with each other and forgive one another if any of you has a grievance against someone. Forgive as the

Lord forgave you. And over all these virtues put on love, which binds them all together in perfect unity" (Colossians 3:12-14). That's a description of someone who is committed to restore those who feel condemned, dirty, and hopeless. Does our frequent Bible study, prayer, and service make us feel self-righteous because we believe we're better than those who don't do those things as often? Or are they disciplines that drive us to Jesus, tenderizing our hearts and giving us compassion for people who are struggling? That's what happened to Paul.

For me, the benchmark of leadership is this: My influence on people may not actually restore them, but I don't want to add to their pain! It's my version of the Hippocratic oath; "First, do no harm." Yeah, that's a low bar, but it's not a bad starting point.

Jesus put His finger on true spirituality in His analogy of the log and the speck. He began with one of the most misunderstood verses in the Bible: "Do not judge, or you too will be judged" (Matthew 7:1). It's popular today to stop people who are giving critiques of any kind by quoting this verse, but it can't mean that we aren't allowed to distinguish good from bad and better from worse. Jesus did that all the time! Instead, it means that we make value judgments without harsh condemnation. He then takes us into His analogy to show how this works:

> "Why do you look at the speck of sawdust in your brother's eye and pay no attention to the plank in your own eye? How can you say to your brother, 'Let me take the speck out of your eye,' when all the time there is a plank in your own eye? You hypocrite, first take the plank out of your own eye, and then you will see clearly to remove the speck from your brother's eye" (vv. 3-5).

I see a lot of people who are blinded by logs who nevertheless insist on trying to take specks out of other people's eyes . . . sometimes with a crowbar! I want to focus on two principles: First, we're qualified to help someone who has a speck only after a loving, patient, skilled friend has helped clear up our vision. Second, taking a speck out of someone's eye requires fine motor skills and a tissue or tweezers. We're not chopping firewood; we're doing delicate eye surgery. This is why we study the Bible, which helps provide direction to our prayers. This is the heart of Jesus for His body of believers, and it's the essence of genuine spirituality.

In every organization and on every team, leaders are reproducing something. Are we creating more people who are long on obedience to various disciplines but short on knowing how to love people well? When the Spirit of God is at work, our impact on the people we lead looks like the relationship between Jesus and Paul.

THE ROLES

It's helpful to delineate the three roles involved in the process of restoring someone: your job, the Holy Spirit's job, and the person's job. We are responsible to but not for. This means we love people with open hands and full hearts, but it's not up to us to force an outcome. To love this way, we need to do whatever it takes to get the log out of our eye and develop the skills to gently, carefully take the speck out of another's.

The Holy Spirit's role is to enable people to "come to their senses"—to want to change, to be open to the process, and see real progress. This isn't a "holy zap." The Spirit most often works through people who are prepared and willing to step into the mess others have created or endured.

The Spirit does the deep, internal work of whispering that the person is God's beloved child, shines a light into the closets, gives assurance that life can be so much bigger and better, and empowers genuine change.

People who are hurting are in the driver's seat, deciding when and how to move forward . . . or not. They do a cost-benefit analysis at every step, and hopefully find the courage to keep making progress during the early stages of change when everything that seemed so right is exposed as so wrong, up seems down and down seems up, and they're feeling more pain instead of less. This terribly awkward period is pivotal, and many decide it's not worth it to keep going. But those who push through the doubts and confusion find a more vibrant life on the other side.

Leaders can schedule the first two stages of relating and trusting, but when people move into the stage of disclosure, the initiative passes to the other person. It's often a waiting game. If we're impatient and try to rush it, we usually get resistance. In this stage, it's important to have frank conversations and ask questions like, "How do you see my role at this point?" "You've told me some important things. What do you want to be different in your life?" "Disclosure is entirely up to you, but do you want me to ask when and if you're ready to talk again?"

I'm very circumspect from this point forward. If people don't take the initiative to schedule time to talk more deeply, I may ask, "Are we good?" but I don't probe at all. And if they want to talk, I pick up where we left off last time and ask something like this: "How have you thought and felt about what you shared with me when we met before?" And I listen. If they're gaining insights, I affirm those and celebrate with them. If they're stuck, I ask a question or two, but I realize it's not up to me to drag them forward.

CREATING A CULTURE

Every organization has a culture, ranging from wonderfully positive to terribly toxic. The New Testament church, and the one that grew out of it that spread through the Roman Empire over the following three centuries, was a healing community—both literally and figuratively. Early critics of the Christians didn't understand their theology, but they marveled at their love. When massive plagues killed about a quarter of the population throughout the empire in the second and third centuries, the Christians risked their lives to care for their pagan neighbors. The church grew because people saw love in action.[36] More recently, the COVID-19 pandemic has given us a taste of what it means to step into the lives of our neighbors to provide compassion and care.

I've rejoiced in seeing the culture change in our church, but not because that was our primary goal. It was more a result of our team of "lions" courageously walking together in honesty and trust. I thought it would take years to change the nature of our church, but it happened far more quickly than I anticipated. Love wins. As the people on our team have gone through the stages I've laid out in this book, they've taken their experiences to their teams and small groups throughout the church. We enjoy each other, we enjoy our roles, and we enjoy seeing the widening impact of compassion throughout our church and our community. Here are a few comments from people on our team of lions:

- *When I came to Rez, Jonathan offered more than a paycheck; he offered friendship. I really wanted a mentor, and he was glad to be that person in my life. Our relationship has been incredible, and it has made a difference. I'm a better husband, a better dad, and a better team member. I'm using the process with people on my team, and it's been phenomenal. They want to own their relational health, and our relationships have been life-giving to all of us.*

- *When I first heard Jonathan talk about the process, I thought, "This is really great. I don't need it, but I know a lot of people who do." As we got into it, I realized I wasn't as far along as I thought. When we got to the Disclose stage, I saw that I'd been managing symptoms all my life, and I'd never gotten below the surface to understand why I'd tried so hard to hide what was really going on in my heart. I wasn't sure I wanted to look at my "dark side," but as I watched other people on the team heal and grow, I wanted the same thing to happen to me. I've experienced healing I didn't even realize I needed. My marriage is stronger, I'm a happier person, and I'm more excited than ever before about my role at the church.*

- *Our team has a really strong network of friendships, and each of us, I think, has a really close friend here. I'm taking my friend through the process, and Jonathan is coaching me as I lead other people.*

- *I had two opposing reactions to the process Jonathan has offered us. I really wanted it, but I was afraid of what I'd find as I went deeper. I've always thought of myself as a pretty emotionally healthy guy, but I found some hurts I'd buried for a long time. Becoming more perceptive and vulnerable is uncomfortable, and sometimes I want to run from it, but I'm experiencing love and healing more than I ever imagined was possible. There's no other place I'd rather be. A defining moment came when I realized I had nothing to fear from Jonathan because he never punishes anyone. He speaks truth and corrects me when I need it, but it's never with a spirit of condemnation. This fear comes from my childhood experiences, but Jonathan dissolves the fear* in love. He often says, "Let's get to the heart of this and resolve it so you can be free."

- Before I came to Rez, I'd never been on a team that values vulnerability. In fact, if anyone had pushed it, I would have run away or never said a word. But Jonathan has been very patient to explain each step, and his demeanor communicates authentic care for us. Since I've been on the team, I've seen that this is a proven model to build relational equity, but only because it's led well.

- I've talked to friends, I've read articles, and I've heard stories of church leaders who are experiencing a lot of stress. And some are so discouraged that they're leaving the ministry. I don't want to be one of them! We who are leaders can't do what God has called us to do—especially over the long haul—if we don't resolve our anxieties through supportive relationships. We need the release valve when we're stressed, and we need the salve of love to keep us going. Sadly, for many people who work for churches, the very last place they find that love and support is with other leaders at their churches. This has to change.

- At my previous church, I often felt like just an employee, but here at Rez, Jonathan has always treated me like a friend and a valuable member of the team. To him, this isn't another program to help the church grow. He genuinely cares about us, and the result is that we're happier, more motivated, and more effective . . . and the church is growing.

- As Jonathan has developed a great friendship with me, I've developed far better relationships with everybody else in my life—especially my wife and my children. If that's the only reason for implementing this process, it's well worth it. But of course, the impact goes far beyond *my sphere of family, friends, and coworkers. Each of them is having a positive influence on the people in their lives, too.*

If I've realized one thing from implementing this process so far, it's that its success starts with me. If I don't consistently and conscientiously practice what I'm presenting, I won't be a help to anyone. This realization is both a humbling responsibility and a high privilege. I know how hard it is to dredge up the gunk of a lifetime and expose it to the light of someone's love, so when one of the lions I walk with takes a step and shares a painful insight, I say, "Bro, you're my hero." And he is.

In our country, we often say that someone with emotional and relational problems "has a lot of baggage," but in Brazil, the word for baggage has a dual meaning. It can have the same connotation of accumulated problems, but it can also mean that a person simply has a lot of experience in a certain area of life that has equipped him to help others who are wrestling with similar difficulties. In that sense, it's associated with wisdom and respect. I started out carrying a lot of harmful and painful baggage from my childhood, but thankfully, over time, God has given me the Portuguese definition of my baggage. He has equipped me to care for others who live with a faint hope that He might turn their tears into joy and their desert into a garden. God delights to redeem our heartaches so we can help people whose hearts are broken.

> "WHEN A BONE IS BROKEN, IT HURTS. BUT IF IT'S SET PROPERLY AND GIVEN TIME TO HEAL, THE BROKEN PLACE WILL BECOME THE STRONGEST PART OF THE BONE. YOU CAN BE STRONGER BECAUSE YOU WERE BROKEN."
> — miss molly —

Believe it. It's true.

↳ WITH ZACH & SETHRY
JUNE 11, 2020

miss MOLLY

SAM AND ME →
ROCKY MOUNTAIN STATE PARK
DEC. 29, 2015

BILLY HORNSBY

THE LIONS → ALL DRESSED UP

SEAN WHEELER AND HIS WIFE SUSAN

1

In your darkest moments, have you had someone who noticed you and "remembered your name"? If you have, what did that person's love mean to you? If not, describe the empty feeling.

....

....

....

....

....

....

....

....

2

Describe what it takes to be "skilled at restoration."

....

....

....

....

....

....

....

....

3

In the matrix of caring
connections, describe
the roles that you,
the Holy Spirit, and
the person play.
How have you seen
these roles become
confused in some
relationships? What
was the damage?
How can you clarify
these roles in your
own mind and in your
communication with
those you lead?

....

....

....

....

....

....

....

....

....

....

4

What steps will
you take to create
a caring culture?

....

....

....

....

....

....

....

....

5

What are the three most
important principles
you've gained from this
book? How are you
applying them (or how
will you apply them)?

....

....

....

....

....

....

....

....

....

....

....

....

....

....

....

....

....

....

....

ENDNOTES

1   Timothy Keller, *The Meaning of Marriage* (New York: Penguin Books, 2011), p. 101.

2   Sadie Dingfelder, "Psychologist testifies on the risks of solitary confinement," APA, October 2012,
https://www.apa.org/monitor/2012/10/solitary

3   C. S. Lewis, *The Four Loves* (New York: HarperCollins, 1960), p. 155.

4   Tommy Walker, "A Worship Minute," http://worship-with-us.org/wp-content/uploads/2012/11/
A-Worship-Minute-May-18th-2014.pdf

5   "The health benefits of strong relationships," *Harvard Health Publishing*, August 6, 2019,
https://www.health.harvard.edu/newsletter_article/the-health-benefits-of-strong-relationships

6   Liz Mineo, "Good genes are nice, but joy is better," *The Harvard Gazette*, April 11, 2017, https://news.harvard.edu/
gazette/story/2017/04/over-nearly-80-years-harvard-study-has-been-showing-how-to-live-a-healthy-and-happy-life/

7   Augustine, *On the Trinity* (Book IX), New Advent, https://www.newadvent.org/fathers/130109.htm

8   This is a summary of the nature of true friendships described by Tim Keller in his message, "Friendship," posted
December 18, 2015, http://reformedevangelist.blogspot.com/2015/12/a-transcription-of-tim-kellers_18.html

9   See "Common Family Roles," https://www.innerchange.com/parents-resources/family-roles/

10   See "What Is Cognitive Behavioral Therapy?" https://www.apa.org/ptsd-guideline/patients-and-families/
cognitive-behavioral

11   See "The Drama Triangle," https://www.metasysteme-coaching.eu/english/the-drama-triangle/

12   Dan Allender, *The Wounded Heart* (Colorado Springs: NavPress, 1990).

13   Martin Luther, *St. Paul's Epistle to the Galatians* (Philadelphia: Smith, English & Co., 1860), p. 206.

14   *Pleasantville*, IMDb review, https://www.imdb.com/title/tt0120789/

15   For instance, see "Loneliness and Addiction," Gateway Foundation, https://www.gatewayfoundation.org/
addiction-blog/loneliness-and-addiction/

16   Lloyd I. Sederer, MD, "What Does 'Rat Park' Teach Us about Addiction?" *Psychiatric Times*, June 10, 2019,
https://www.psychiatrictimes.com/view/what-does-rat-park-teach-us-about-addiction

17   Adapted from "Friendship," Tim Keller. https://gospelinlife.com/downloads/friendship-5396/

18   Stephanie Dyrness Lobdell, "When You're a Pastor Who Suffers from Depression," *Christianity Today*, December
2017, https://www.christianitytoday.com/pastors/2017/december-web-exclusives/
when-youre-pastor-who-suffers-from-depression.html

19   "Clergy More Likely to Suffer from Depression, Anxiety," Duke Today Staff,
https://today.duke.edu/2013/08/clergydepressionnewsrelease

20   "Seasonal affective disorder explained," Mayo Clinic, January 16 2018, https://www.mayoclinichealthsystem.org/
        hometown-health/speaking-of-health/seasonal-affective-disorder-explained

21   Diane Gleim, "No One Is Immune to Sexual Shame," *Psychology Today*, August 20, 2019,
        https://www.psychologytoday.com/us/blog/underneath-the-sheets/201908/no-one-is-immune-sexual-shame

22   Cited by Les Parrott in *Crazy Good Sex* (Grand Rapids: Zondervan, 2009), p. 46.

23   Stephanie Coontz, "Generation X and millennials may have found a new secret to sexual happiness," *Washington Post*,
        August 5, 2016, https://www.washingtonpost.com/opinions/less-sex-more-satisfaction/2016/08/05/
        08a41af0-5b46-11e6-831d-0324760ca856_story.html

24   Machiavelli, *The Prince* (Cambridge: Cambridge University Press, 1988), p. 54, adapted.

25   J. I. Packer, *Knowing God* (Downers Grove: InterVarsity Press, 1973), p. 221.

26   Kim Scott, author of *Radical Candor* (New York: St. Martin's Press, 2017)
        https://www.radicalcandor.com/our-approach/

27   "Friendship," *Stanford Encyclopedia of Philosophy*, 2005, https://plato.stanford.edu/entries/friendship/

28   C. S. Lewis, *The Four Loves* (New York: HarperOne, 2017), pp. 96-97.

29   Brad Meltzer, *The Inner Circle* (New York: Grand Central Publishing, 2011), p. 125.

30   Emma Seppälä, "What Bosses Gain by Being Vulnerable," *Harvard Business Review*, December 11, 2014,
        https://hbr.org/2014/12/what-bosses-gain-by-being-vulnerable

31   Robert M. Kaplan and Dennis P. Saccuzzo, *Psychological Testing* (Pacific Grove, California: Brooks/Cole Publishing
        Company, 1989), pp. 445-447.

32   Ann Voskamp, *The Way of Abundance* (Grand Rapids: Zondervan, 2018), p. 94.

33   Henri J. M. Nouwen, *The Wounded Healer* (New York: Doubleday, 1979), pp. 72, 41.

34   William Shakespeare, *The Merchant of Venice*, Act IV, Scene I.

35   T. S. Eliot, *Four Quartets* (New York: Houghton Mifflin Harcourt, 1943), p. 47.

36   For much more on the Christians' response during these plagues, see Rodney Stark's
        The Triumph of Christianity (New York: HarperOne, 2011).

ACKNOWLEDGEMENTS

AMY

Thank you for loving me and supporting me, my dreams, and my journey of healing and growth. Thank you for graciously and powerfully leading the women on our team through this process. You are the bravest person I know. I love you!

MY KIDS AND FAMILY

Thanks to my kids, Nathan, Madelyn, Sarah, and Sam, my daughter-in-law Madalynn Rose, and my grandson Johnny. Pray I sell a ton of books. Your inheritance depends on it! You are my favorites!

DON AND LINDA BOYETT

Thanks for showing me what a lifetime of faithfulness to God and each other looks like. You truly are my heroes. I want to be just like you when I grow up.

REZ.CHURCH

To my church, thank you for supporting me and my family through thick and thin. We love you, Rez!

PASTOR GREG SURRATT

Thanks for truly being a pastor to me and countless others. You have built quite a legacy by faithfully adding value to the successes of those you mentor and building the legacies of so many others for the cause of Christ. You easily share credit while happily shouldering responsibility—both are essential characteristics for great leaders. And you are a great leader.

DINO RIZZO

Thanks to you and ARC for believing in me enough to generously provide a platform for this book. You've opened many doors for me, and my world is bigger for it. You're one of a kind!

PAT SPRINGLE

You're a remarkably intelligent and soulful writer who helped me write this book. I couldn't have done this without you!

SUSAN AND STEVE BLOUNT

You are excellent, ethical, enthusiastic, and capable. You add value to many parts of the Body of Christ and many streams of ministry in many ways. If the scope of your contribution was truly recognized, yours would be household names for people of faith everywhere.

LANDON HAIRGROVE

Thanks for not letting me do anything without giving it my very best efforts. You're a force of nature for good in this world. You cheer me on as if my success is your success. Your wisdom and character are rare, especially considering your young age. Because of your talent stack and formidable skill set, you could easily choose to be self-sufficient, but instead, you've chosen to live in and for a community that enriches you and is enriched by you. Thanks for being one of the lions in my life.

TY BELLMORE

Thank you for being a caring and intentional friend on a world-class level and for encouraging me to write this book in the first place. Thanks for being one of the lions in my life.

JOSHUA BOYETT

You're my friend and my brother. You never lose sight of the value of each person you encounter. You honor people as a way of life. I admire you for that. Thanks for being one of the lions in my life.

JAMES MERKLEY

You've taught me to invest my life in the ways that maximize an eternal return. You're a remarkable friend, leader, husband, and human. You ask the best questions! You have my profound respect. Thanks for being one of the lions in my life.

JEREMY WEINLAND

You are a disarmingly kind and ridiculously gifted leader. You have a depth of capacity and heart, and I'd follow you into battle. You show up for people time and time again. Thanks for being one of the lions in my life.

SAMUEL BRUM

You're a pioneering, faithful, and prophetic leader, and you're doing incredible things in Brazil. You're an enduring friend who always finds ways to encourage and inspire people around you. No one on earth is funnier than you, bro! Thanks for being one of the lions in my life.

MARCUS LEE ROBINSON

You've become a voice for the disenfranchised, the vulnerable, and the fatherless. I wish you every success. Thank you for being one of the lions in my life.

ISAIAH HUPP

You've taken steps toward growth that were, at times, counterintuitive for you. Still, you chose to not only move forward toward growth and trust, but to multiply that culture and vision in the hearts of many others. You lead with the best of them. Thanks for being one of the lions in my life.

ZACH SANCHEZ

I've watched you grow through this process with an uncommon level of courage and intentionality. You've faced your obstacles and conquered them one by one. Never in a hurry, you move forward purposefully and at a sustainable pace, choosing to trust with your eyes wide open. Thank you for being my good friend, a courageous lion, and at times, my travel buddy, too.

ANDREW CONNOR

Your life portrays excellence from every conceivable vantage point. Your character, attitude, loyalty, self-discipline, care, and example are above reproach. You bring an incomparable level of excellence into our friendship. You inspire me. There is simply no one else like you, my friend. Thanks for being one of the lions in my life.

ZACH CRIDER

You're one of the best leaders and friends I've ever known. Thank you for challenging me to never waste my vulnerability and to relentlessly pursue my dreams with courage, resourcefulness, and grit. You make everyone around you better. From silly jokes to ancient poetry, you have incredible range to be a warrior/king/shepherd/songwriter kind of leader. You know, you're basically like King David! Thanks for being one of the lions in my life. Love you, my friend.

THERE ARE SOME PEOPLE I JUST WOULDN'T WANT TO DO LIFE WITHOUT:

Adam Braud, Simeon Myers, Joel Bodker, Matthew Barnett, Nate Puccini, Seth Baltzell, Brian Carpenter, Ray Ferrell, Luciano Subira, Israel Subira, Wayne Hilsden, Dave Sumrall, Kim Walker-Smith, Skyler Smith, Emily Boyett, Mike Olson, Keith and Lori Malone, Randall Wiggins, Josh Joines, Jason Parrish, Paul Andrew, Greg Daley, Darryn Scheske. and Cornelius Lindsey,

SETHRY CONNOR

Finally, I want to express my profound gratitude to my best friend and a co-laborer in ministry, Sethry Connor. You are my "friend born for times of adversity" who "sticks closer than a brother." Your contribution to this work and to my life has made me a better husband, father, leader, and friend. I learned a ton of the principles in this book from you. You're the most generous, brilliant, articulate, intelligent, capable, genuine, and all-around best person I know. You are the OG Lion!

ABOUT
THE
AUTHOR

Jonathan Wiggins

Jonathan Wiggins grew up in northern Louisiana. He graduated from the University of Louisiana at Monroe with a degree in economics and a concentration in finance. He has served as the worship leader for a number of organizations, beginning with King's Camp in Mer Rouge, Louisiana, for sixteen summers, where he also served as a counselor and camp director. For five years, he was the worship leader at City of Faith Halfway House, a ministry providing nonviolent offenders opportunities to be grounded in faith, find work, and reenter society after imprisonment. For ten years, he served as the worship leader at Providence Church in Lake Providence, and for five years, he served at First Baptist Church in West Monroe. He has been at Rez.Church for twelve years, two as the worship leader and ten as the lead pastor.

The church, originally called Loveland Assembly of God, was founded in 1915. The name was changed to Resurrection Fellowship, but since everyone called it Rez, they officially changed the name to Rez.Church. In the last few years, the thriving church Jonathan inherited has launched multiple locations. Today Rez locations are at the hub of current and projected demographic growth of the northern tier of the Front Range of Colorado.

Rez is known for its dynamic worship, anointed preaching, excellence of ministry, and a passion for the world. Since 1999, the church has given over $1,000,000 annually to compassion and outreach works around the world with a special focus on Israel. In 1998, Rez founded Resurrection Christian School, beginning with an elementary school wing. Today RCS has grown to more than 1400 students, preschool through 12th grade, and is the largest Christian school in Northern Colorado.

Jonathan has spoken at events throughout the country, but is most excited about his annual trips to Brazil to speak at churches and conferences, partnering with his friend Luciano Subira and the Portuguese-language House of Zadok. He is a member of the executive board of the Fellowship of Israel Related Ministries, FIRM. He also began a statewide initiative, Nothing

Without God, to partner with church plants in Colorado. This ministry provides digital resources for leaders who want to deepen relationships inside and outside their churches.

He met Amy at King's Camp when they were about nine years old. He says, "Every summer I fell in love with her again." They officially began dating when he was sixteen, and they married when he was twenty-one, which was twenty-four years ago. They have four children. Nathan is in college, majoring in political science and president of the poly-sci club. He's married to Maddy, and they have a son, Johnny. Their daughter Mady is a gifted communicator on social media and plans to be part of the launch team for Rez.Church in Rio de Janeiro. Sarah, a dancer and actor, just graduated from high school. Their youngest, Sam, is an athlete, currently focused on playing on the golf team at his school.

Jonathan admits that he's not very good at golf, but he enjoys Topgolf. He sometimes finds himself fly fishing in the streams and rivers of Colorado, Montana, and Utah, and he spends as much time as possible hiking trails in the Rockies. He and his family camp in the mountains, and they are "fans of everything Disney."

Association of Related Churches

We are a global family of church and business leaders that exists to see a thriving church in every community reaching people with the message of Jesus. We do this by providing relationships, resources, and opportunities to leaders of new and existing churches so that they can thrive.

WE LAUNCH

We have a highly successful, proven model for planting churches with a big launch day to gain the initial momentum needed to plant a church. We train church planters, and we provide a tremendous boost in resources needed.

WE CONNECT

We provide dozens of opportunities to connect with other church planters, veteran pastors, leadership mentors, as well as friends who are walking the same path as you are. You're never short on opportunities to connect!

WE EQUIP

Our team continually creates and collects great ministry resources that will help you and your church be the best you can be. As part of this family, you get to draw water from a deep well of experience in ministry.

LAUNCHING, CONNECTING, & EQUIPPING THE LOCAL CHURCH

To find resources on church planting, books, articles, stories, webinars, partner organizations, and more, visit

EQUIP.ARCCHURCHES.COM

arc RESOURCES
HOW-TO SERIES

SERVE YOUR CITY by Dino Rizzo

Through the pages of the Gospels, we see Jesus model a "show and tell" like and ministry to His followers—He "showed" them how to serve by healing the sick, feeding the hungry, and caring for the poor—and while He was demonstrating compassion, He taught them, "telling" them of God's immense love. This is the way to break down barriers so people will listen to the life-changing message of the gospel of grace.

In *Serve Your City*, you'll sense Dino Rizzo's heart, be inspired by his stories, and learn from his experiences, as well as many ARC churches that are serving their cities with a Jesus-style, no-strings-attached kind of love. This is at the core of who ARC is—a deep passion to see churches thrive as part of the cities they serve.

RE-VISIONING by Greg Surratt

Vision. It can be a very slippery thing. As leaders, we can have a crystal-clear sense of purpose and direction at some points, but they may seem like foreign objects from time to time. Sooner or later, it happens to all of us. In this book, Pastor Greg Surratt shares his story of asking himself hard questions . . . and finding the answers to be both surprising and inspiring. He addresses the crucial topics of limitations, culture, and legacy, but he also dives into harder issues of how to handle heartaches and what actually captures the hearts of the people we lead.

Re-Visioning is designed to recharge our leadership batteries and equip us to inspire our teams with humility, boldness, and joy. Greg is a pioneer in church planting and multi-site strategy. Leaders in all sizes of churches and across the spectrum of denominations value his insights, his heart, and his blend of kindness and tenacity in advancing God's kingdom.